Jezebel

A PORTRAIT OF SIN

JEREMIAH BOLICH

Cross Style Press™

Jezebel: A Portrait of Sin

Second Edition

ISBN: 9780615760711

Additional copies may be ordered from:

Jeremiah Bolich Ministries
PO Box 2089
Lebanon, TN 37088

www.JeremiahBolich.com

TABLE OF CONTENTS

INTRODUCTION

Jezebel

INTRODUCTION

I'm not sure if everyone feels as I do, but there have been numerous times throughout my life when I sought the approval of others. And just when I think I've outgrown this kind of pressure, I find myself seeking it again.

As a young man in my early twenties who had been called to ministry, I desperately wanted to "get it right." Until that time, I had gotten most things wrong. When I looked back at my life prior to Christ, I remember seeing someone numbed with drugs and alcohol, who was probably let out of high school rather than graduating, and who had wasted three years of military service - having been discharged early due to drug use. Beginning with a fresh start as a Christian in ministry was important to me and I simply wanted to get it right.

I must be honest, as I sit here in my home in Watertown, Tennessee writing about how I feel, I chuckle a bit. It was so intimidating to be in college among fellow ministry majors. I felt like the cue ball among pool balls on the billiard table; different than every other minister in my class.

I could go on and on about my past and upbringing, but it is enough to say that I felt I was not minister material. I didn't look like a minister, talk like a minister, and probably didn't act like a minister. So, I set out to prove myself and a major piece in that process was to gain the approval of others. I changed my clothing, my hair, the way I talked, and anything that would make me one of the group. Some of the changes have endured, and probably for the better, but most drifted away as I matured in Christ.

Regardless, here I am again feeling the same way with all the same recognizable pressures. I guess I should confess from the start that I do not feel like a writer. I've never taken a writing class, felt capable with expressing myself through writing, nor read a great many books. I'm a preacher! I stand and preach, not sit and write. I often think to myself, "I probably should leave the writing to those who are gifted to write." Yet the moment that thought comes, I feel the urge and perhaps even the call, to write. For amidst all my conflicting emotions is the Truth that I have found and am driven to share through as many avenues as possible.

OPINIONS VARY

It is true that I have not read a great many books, but I do read. And the authors I've read, including those whose content I've liked and disliked, often times and once again leave me feeling on the outside.

I do not care much for opinions and if there is one thing that turns me off to a writer, it is the one who consistently pushes his or her opinions. I am a man drawn to facts, and even more, to Truth. I don't embrace what has been commonly said, "opinions are like feet, everyone has them and most stink," but I would contend that Truth always supersedes opinions.

This is how I want to write this book. I want to present to you not my own opinions, or the opinions of others, but the Truth I've found in the Bible. If you are not a Christian and do not hold that the Bible is the inspired Word of God, then everything you find in this book will be less for you than what I desire. If you are a Christian, however, you will recognize immediately that I am not giving you my opinion, slant, spin, or interpretation, but simply showing you what has already been written.

In this way, I am still a preacher, only writing what I've found rather than speaking it. And to me, it is a warm blanket on a cold night. In many ways it alleviates and even liberates me from criticism. For I did not produce or conjure up this material, but simply retell what has already been told.

This is an important aspect to this book and I feel that you, as the reader, should know my heart from the beginning. Although I may illustrate throughout the book how this Truth has changed me personally, the Truth that has changed me did not originate in me. It did not come from my experience, intellect, or from any other man.

Therefore I would ask that you tolerate, if you occasionally get bored with my word studies and cultural explanations, the style in which I have chosen to write. It is necessary. Please be patient and consider what I have found.

NOT A COMMENTARY

I am fortunate in that two of my best friends from college married my wife's two sisters. There's just something about getting your buddies in the family. Dave and Chad have been my friends, advisors, and accountability partners over the years, so when I asked them to preview some of this book, I was prepared to get an honest and straightforward response. What I was not prepared for was their accusation that it read like a commentary. I use "accusation" and not "perspective" because my intent was never to write a commentary.

Now it must be said that I would not be opposed for this book to be used as a commentary. There are certainly benefits that it could render for those who seek to study Revelation 2:18-29. The intent of this book, however, is not to sit on a minister's reference shelf or be used strictly for the college classroom, but for any Christian who desires to know more about the life of a child of God.

NOT FLUFF

The dictionary on my computer defines fluff as: *"Entertainment or writing perceived as trivial or superficial: the movie is a piece of typical Hollywood fluff."*

This next year I turn forty and I am beginning to notice that many of the words and illustrations I use tell my age more than I would like. *Fluff* is one of those telling words. I don't hear it used much anymore, but I'd like to bring it back into circulation. It is a good word and serves my purpose in this context to describe how I don't want this book to be received.

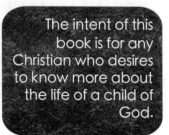

The intent of this book is for any Christian who desires to know more about the life of a child of God.

Whenever a person considers becoming a Christian, more is at stake for that person than simple lifestyle changes. This seems to be a common misunderstanding among some Christians. When a person embraces the message of the Gospel, accepts Jesus as their personal savior, and then is filled with God Himself, that person does not simply begin doing different things, they become a different person. Paul writes in 2 Corinthians 5:17,

"Therefore, if anyone is in Christ, he is a new creation; the old has gone, the new has come."

He writes on this issue again to the church in Galatia, addressing how certain Jews boast about their religious actions. Galatians 6:15 reads,

"Neither circumcision nor uncircumcision means anything; what counts is a new creation."

I became a new creation in 1995. I had recently been discharged from active duty from the Marine Corps and was living in southern California. In those early days of Faith, I remember the sharp contrast between who I was and what I had become. I felt different. I processed life differently. I was different!

The Bible is very clear on what I was experiencing then and what I still experience today. David writes in Psalm 32:8,

"God will instruct me and teach me in the way I should go. He will guide me with His eye."

David's son Solomon writes much the same way throughout the book of Proverbs. In Proverbs 3:5-6 he writes,

When a person embraces the message of the Gospel, accepts Jesus as their personal savior, and then is filled with God Himself, that person does not simply begin doing different things, they become a different person.

"I trust in the Lord with all my heart and lean not on my own understanding. In all my ways I acknowledge Him and He directs my paths."

Of course, God's activity only intensifies in the New Covenant when God moves from being outside His servants to living inside His children. In John 16:13 Jesus tells his disciples,

"But when He, the Spirit of Truth, comes, He will guide you into all Truth. He will not speak on His own; He will

speak only what He hears, and He will tell you what is yet to come."

Christians, therefore, are new creations, not because they are changed into perfection, making no mistakes and free of any faults, but because they have God Himself dwelling within them. We no longer operate independently from God, but respond to His leading and guidance in our life. We are no longer self-led, but God-directed.

This is what moves Christianity beyond the fluff of a religious life. Religion informs an individual on how they are to act and how they are to live. It provides rules and guidelines for a specific lifestyle, most of the time reflecting devotion to a god or system of belief. Christianity, on the other hand, is altogether different. A Christian does not live in response to rules or guidelines per se, rather while living in intimacy with Jesus through the indwelling presence of His Spirit, experiences life through the eyes of God Himself.

It has been seventeen years since I became a new creation. I have grown a little older, have a bit of gray, and have also grown spiritually. Many of the ways in which I used to live and think have changed, but not simply because I have gained more information. The changes in my life have taken place in response to my Lord and Savior Jesus Christ. As He leads, I follow. When He speaks, I respond. I live differently because I am different.

HOUSE, SIMON COWELL, AND WALT KOWALSKI

Some say that the 50's was the generation where "cool" was invented. So if you've never heard of the Fanz or Elvis Presley, you need to google them and see if you agree. These two icons give insight into the socially popular of that generation.

Today's culture is very different and, therefore, has different icons who represent what is considered "cool." House, Simon Cowell, and the testy old Korean war vet in the movie Grand Torino, Walt Kowalski, seem to resonate with many in today's culture. These men, whether real life icons or fictional characters, are prime examples of those who are believed to possess the "cool" trait.

What defining characteristic earns them this elite status? They are upfront; they are bold; and despite being at times rude, harsh, and uncaring, they are brutally honest. They are representatives of a generation who "come out of the closet" to be real, not only with boldness, but with flair. They represent a culture that chooses to be real regardless of the cost.

15

As I've already stated, I do not embrace every opinion and walk of life. However I do embrace being being upfront and honest, whatever the cost. That's just the way the vast majority of my generation and I approach life. It saturates our entertainment, values, and even our belief systems.

I see this consistently as I travel from church to church across the nation. People want to know the Truth! They want whatever message I bring laid out plain and simple. People are tired of politics, smooth talking, and the smoke and mirrors approach in which many preachers fall victim. Regardless of what they believe, or whether they believe or not, they want to know what I believe, plain and simple.

After the surprise of having to give a "sex talk" to teenagers at a teen camp in New York State a few years ago, I sat in the guy's discussion group. The director had divided the teens into two groups, girls and guys, to get their reaction to the session. I was intrigued by one guy in particular. We'll call him Tommy.

Tommy was upfront and honest about the session; he was not a fan of abstinence. He shared that he enjoyed having sex with his girlfriend, how it made them closer and more secure, and he wasn't interested in changing their relationship.

Despite the intensity of the group and the seriousness of the discussion, I found the scene comical. After an hour of pleading and even threatening, Tommy would not bend on his stance. With hesitation, after a look from the director, I addressed Tommy with the same boldness that he himself used in expressing the sexual relationship between he and his girlfriend.

I told Tommy that it appeared he was not interested in being a Christian. From what he had said, it was evident that the Christian life did not suit him. I then gave him the out that he was not looking for when I told him that his decision was his own and we would honor it by not forcing our views upon him. Yet this discussion was for Christians, and since he did not want to be one, he did not have to participate any longer.

I can still remember the shock of the director and the murderous looks of both the teens and parents who had showed up for the evening service. But what stood out to me the most was the look on Tommy's face. He was clearly uncomfortable with abandoning the Christian Faith. I gathered from his expression, that it was one thing to be a little edgy and somewhat rebellious, and another thing to reject being a Christian.

As the week continued, I purposefully eluded Tommy and brushed off his inquiries to sit and chat. I told him that I did not want to guilt him into being a Christian and that I was fine with his decision. I told him, "It's cool man, you don't have to be a Christian. Live it up dude."

By mid week, Tommy was a wreck! It was quite funny! He had been playing the "bad boy" card and liked the attention, but was coming to the conclusion that it would cost him more than he wanted to pay. Tommy believed what he heard that week, and deep inside, knew he wanted to follow Christ. So, on the second to the last night of camp, Tommy recommitted his life to Jesus and surrendered his "bad boy" image to Jesus.

What is so "cool" about this aggressive approach to Tommy, is that it did not originate with House, Simon, or Walt; Jesus Himself invented this approach. There are countless examples in the Bible where Jesus told people, "count the cost." In Luke 14:28-33, Jesus reasons with the onlooking crowd to count the cost of following Him. He says,

"Suppose one of you wants to build a tower. Will he not first sit down and estimate the cost to see if he has enough money to complete it?"

And again He says,

"Or suppose a king is about to go to war against another king. Will he not first sit down and consider whether he is able with ten thousand men to oppose the one coming against him with twenty thousand?"

Jesus was upfront, honest, and aggressive with those who would embrace the radical call to follow Him. He used no deception and did not dazzle people with smoke and mirrors. As demonstrated in His confrontation with the Rich Young Ruler, Jesus spoke boldly and without hesitation to His generation.

Without question, the content of this book is aggressive; therefore, it is aggressively written. As my mammy would say, in this book, there will be no "beating around the bush."

It is my desire that as you move through this book, you will consider Jesus' perspective on sin and how that perspective changes your life personally.

SIN

This book revolves around the topic of sin and specifically from the viewpoint of Jesus' address to the church in Thyatira, found in Revelation 2:18-29. We will explore and consider the language Jesus uses to describe sin and compare it to the language used by many religious and Christian people today. We will also discuss the origin, physical affects, and spiritual consequences of sin.

As we have already established, the content of this book is weighty, which is certainly true of sin. There would seem to be no other word used by religious or Christian people that is as divisive as the word *sin*. Whenever the topic comes up, words like *judgemental, guilty, hurt, perfect,* and *angry* seem to follow. Therefore, it can safely be said that sin is not usually a pleasant conversation piece. Yet, as we shall see in this book, Jesus addresses the subject nonetheless.

It is my desire that as you move through this book, you will consider Jesus' perspective on sin and how that perspective changes your life personally. For each and every human being, the topic of sin is a matter of life or death. It is my desire and great hope, after walking through the analysis of Jesus' address to Thyatira, that we would gain a more Christ-like perspective of sin and live free of the slavery that it causes.

KEY CONCEPTS

Whenever the Christian Faith is discussed, opinions must come under the Bible's authority.

Having a fluent knowledge of the Bible is crucial to living the Christian life. This requires more from a believer than simply doing devotions. Every Christian should engage as often as possible in a serious and deliberate study of the Bible.

Every Christian should be prepared to give reasons why they believe what the Bible says.

The opinions and reason of mankind are always subject to the Bible.

Sin is not a trivial matter, but a weighty one. In this word hangs the choice between Heaven and Hell.

REFLECTION QUESTIONS

1. In the casual conversations of life, is it beneficial to correct someone who expresses opinions about Christianity when they are not consistent with the Bible? If not, why? If so, how do you do that?

2. When describing your Faith to non-believers, how do you incorporate the Bible without sounding like your "preaching?" Can you think of an example from your own past experiences?

3. When sharing your Faith, do you feel more like Simon Cowell or the Cowardly Lion? Why?

4. If you did not want to use the word "sin" in a conversation with someone, what other word would you use?

5. Is it worth offending someone in order to be honest with them about a topic as weighty as sin?

LET'S GET TECHNICAL

Jezebel

CHAPTER 1

LET'S GET TECHNICAL

Of all the things I learned during my time in the United States Marine Corps, how to approach the enemy on a battlefield was among the most significant. During boot camp, I learned when approaching an enemy who is firing at me, to repeat the phrase: "I'm up, he sees me, I'm down." Saying this phrase while jumping up, zigzagging across an open field, and diving for cover, would most certainly save my life. My Drill Instructors grilled into me, how one approaches things makes all the difference.

I found it intriguing after studying Jesus' addresses to the seven churches of Revelation chapters two and three, how much emphasis Jesus put on His approach. If you were to stand back and look at Jesus' addresses as a whole, you would find some striking consistencies. Jesus approaches each church in the exact same way. He uses the same format of address, calls for a response, and always promises an outcome.

This is Jesus' approach to each church and He never deviates from it.

The consistencies tucked away in Jesus' approach are so exact that it demands our attention. Jesus uses reoccurring phrases, words, and promises which reach beyond the individual circumstances of each church, to paint an overall perspective that every church would certainly see. This perspective is crucial when trying to understand the message Jesus gives to each church. What is more, this perspective of Jesus' approach lays out for the reader what the Gospel message looks like in the practical, everyday settings of life.

In a first reading, processing all that Jesus speaks to the churches, you will find that each church is very different from the others. Each church has a cultural setting, level of persecution, economic situation, and level of intimacy and devotion to God. Just like today's churches, each is unique and has real people struggling to live in a real world with real problems.

In a second reading, other details of Jesus' address might begin to appear. You might see there is a three-part division to His address. There is an opening introduction of Himself, a revelation of His knowledge to the specific church's context, and a result that He wants to bring about for that church. As we progress through this book, we will see how important each aspect of Jesus' address is to the church in Thyatira, but let's begin here with explaining each part.

The three-part approach Jesus chooses when addressing these churches are:

1. Jesus introduces Himself
2. Jesus speaks of the church's context
3. Jesus desires to produce a result

JESUS INTRODUCES HIMSELF

Jesus' introduces Himself to each church in the exact same manner. In Revelation 2:1, 8, 12, 18; 3:1, 7, and 14 this same expression appears when Jesus begins His introduction.

"To the angel of the church in (church name) write: These are the words of Him who..."

Introductions are important, especially in the Bible. There are countless examples in the Bible where names were specifically given to people to represent what kind of people they were or who they would eventually become. Therefore, those who were introduced to Israel (formerly Jacob, Isaac's son),

Moses, or Peter were receiving more than a generic name, but a title representing the identity of that person. *Israel* was the name that identified Jacob and his descendants as God's child, *Moses* as God's deliverance, and *Peter* as the rock for the newly found Church.

Jesus does the same thing when He introduces Himself to these churches. He does not use His name, but uses specific language to give insight to His identity. What is more, His description is specifically tailored to each church. How He introduces Himself reveals how He intends to minister and interact with that church.

He not only uses this method of introduction for Himself, but at times will give titles to specific people in specific churches. As we will find out later in Jesus' address to Thyatira, He labels a women in their church with the name *Jezebel*. Jezebel is more than likely not her real name, but the title chosen by Jesus to reveal her identity to the church.

JESUS SPEAKS OF THE CHURCH'S CONTEXT

Similarly, with consistent language Jesus enters into the body of His address to each church. Each elaborate description of the church's context always contains the words, "I know." He repeatedly says statements like,

"I know your deeds" and *"I know where you live"*

Jesus knows what is taking place in each church in every city. In fact, He reveals to the churches in Smyrna and Thyatira that He knows more of their context than they do. He knows of Smyrna's Jewish persecution and that they are actually a "synagogue of Satan." To Thyatira, He reveals the true identity of a woman in leadership, labeling her Jezebel.

In the context of each church's day-to-day living, Jesus reveals what is really happening. In His addresses He calls each church to embrace Him and receive comfort, for He knows exactly the physical and spiritual situation each church faces.

JESUS DESIRES TO PRODUCE A RESULT

As the details of each church's context are laid out, Jesus moves to a result that He desires for each church. What Jesus wants to produce is relevant for both the church as a whole as well as each individual in the church. This part of His address always contains the phrases,

"To him who overcomes" and *"He who has an ear, let him hear what the Spirit says to the churches."*

Life-change does not stop the moment we become a Christian; it begins. Although we are certainly a new creation at the moment we believe and are filled with the Holy Spirit, we still mature and grow from a child to an adult in God's family. God will always be our Father and will always mentor and mature us into His fantastic design.

As in the case with Thyatira, sometimes growing takes discipline. Receiving discipline is a fundamental part of being a child of God. The author of Hebrews writes:

"Endure hardship as discipline; God is treating you as sons. For what son is not disciplined by his father? If you are not disciplined (and everyone undergoes discipline), then you are illegitimate children and not true sons. Moreover, we have all had human fathers who disciplined us and we respected them for it. How much more should we submit to the Father of our spirits and live! Our fathers disciplined us for a little while as they thought best; but God disciplines us for our good, that we may share in His holiness. No discipline seems pleasant at the time, but painful. Later on, however, it produces a harvest of righteousness and peace for those who have been trained by it." Hebrews 12:7-11

Therefore, whether by gentle instruction or through difficult discipline, God acts with purpose to bring to pass what He desires for each church.

Each aspect of Jesus' address is layered with precision and purpose. Every word He says and even the way He says it is important. God loves humanity, desiring for none to perish in sin and slavery. This love compels Him to act and save any who would listen and return to Him as children.

As we move through the address to Thyatira, we will consistently pause and consider both what Jesus says to the church and how He says it. There is great truth presented to the church and if we are careful to recognize Jesus' approach, we will not miss what He desires for each and every person in Thyatira.

THE LANGUAGE OF REVELATION

When I began to study the book of Revelation, I felt it was necessary to familiarize myself with its language. This was necessary, for it only takes a quick read-through to realize the language used is not common to modern day readers.

What I discovered, and what many scholars have noted after studying the book, is that much of the language used in Revelation is symbolic. For example,

John's lengthy description of Jesus after He appeared in a vision to him on the island of Patmos, pictures a sword protruding from Jesus' mouth. John writes,

"In His right hand He held seven stars, and out of His mouth came a sharp double-edged sword." (Revelation 1:16a)

And again, writing of the glorious throne room scene in Revelation chapter 5, John describes Jesus as,

"...a Lamb, looking as if it had been slain, standing in the center of the throne, encircled by the four living creatures and the elders." (Revelation 5:6)

These descriptions of Jesus are obviously not literal, so they must carry a symbolic meaning. Jesus, as a human being and not a cyborg or mythical creature, does not have a sword instead of a tongue. He also certainly does not resemble an animal, much less a dead one. These descriptions are symbolic and carry significance beyond their physical meaning.

Yet, there is also language that falls short of symbolic and must be taken literally. In His address to the church in Smyrna, Jesus describes Himself as,

"...the First and the Last, who died and came to life again." (Revelation 2:8)

This is not symbolic, but literal. The Christian Faith not only declares, but hinges on the literal physical death and resurrection of Jesus Christ.

Therefore, with both symbolic and literal language used in Revelation, a dilemma is presented to the reader. When do you understand a statement or scenario as symbolic and when do you understand it literally?

This dilemma becomes considerably less problematic when you interpret the book of Revelation using the Bible.

THE KEY TO SCRIPTURE IS SCRIPTURE

The key to understanding the Bible is the Bible itself. If you attend a Nazarene, Methodist, or Wesleyan church, you are strongly influenced by a man named John Wesley. Wesley's rule for theology, as well as interpreting the Bible, followed four ordered steps: Scripture (Bible), tradition, reason, and then experience. This order of interpretation is commonly known as the Wesleyan Quadrilateral. I believe it is the safest way to interpret the Bible and the only way to make sense of Revelation.

In His introductions, Jesus reaches back into what we call the Old Testament, or Old Covenant Scriptures, and takes words, phrases, and prophecies to convey not only who He is, but God's desired identity for each church.

A perfect example of this is seen when Jesus addresses the church in Philadelphia. Jesus says,

"These are the words of Him who is Holy and True, who holds the key of David." (Revelation 3:7)

The phrase "holds the key of David" is found in Isaiah 22:22, and depicts through God's appointment of a steward, Eliakim son of Hilkiah, both what is seen in Jesus and what God desires for the church in Philadelphia. This is precisely why Jesus uses this phrase to introduce Himself to this church.

Like Eliakim, and yet in perfection, Jesus is a steward. What is more, Jesus is the standard of all stewardship! Jesus gave His life for the

> The key to understanding the Bible is the Bible itself.

purpose and call of God, being the perfect example of what God intends for all His children. Jesus came to seek and save the lost and not to lose any of those whom the Father appointed unto Him. Jesus not only faithfully embraced this call, but is fulfilling it entirely. Thus, Jesus is the perfect steward.

This is the message to the church in Philadelphia, and although Jesus will explain the specific details in the body of His address, He first communicates the stewardship message in the way He introduces Himself. Note that Jesus does not use His name, but instead, reaches into the Scriptures to communicate not only His identity, but the desired identity of those in the church at Philadelphia.

Jesus' address to Philadelphia reveals why utilizing the Old Testament, the only Scripture the early church had at that time, to determine what is literal and what is symbolic, gives tremendous insight into why specific words and phrases are used. Jesus' choice of words are not random but intentional. If we are to understand the message Jesus desires to communicate, then we must interpret His statements in light of the Scriptures.

HIS IDENTITY. OUR IDENTITY

When introducing Himself to the churches of Revelation chapters two and three, Jesus uses both symbolic and literal language to convey a message. Certainly that message reveals His identity to each specific church, but as we have already seen, the message also reveals what each church is to look like.

Jesus' introductions link His own identity with the churches in which He addresses. He purposefully reveals how He identifies with the context of each church in everyday life. He is sympathetic to each church, knowing exactly what they are going through, for He also has lived as they are living. The Bible tells us in Hebrews 4:15,

"For we do not have a high priest who is unable to sympathize with our weaknesses, but we have one who has been tempted in every way, just as we are--yet was without sin."

As a Christian, this fact gives me a comfort that is hard to describe. It is one thing to serve an unrelating god in this world of temptation, heartache, and pain, and another thing entirely to know that Jesus understands my struggles.

I was quite shocked when I first realized that Jesus was a normal, average, everyday man, just like me. Until I really sat down and studied His life, I always considered Jesus more like superman than a normal man. I mean, He walked on water, raised the dead, and knew people's thoughts. Normal people can't do that, can they?

Yet the book of Acts tells of Peter raising the dead (Acts 9:40), Phillip teleporting from here to there (Acts 8:39-40), and nearly every disciple healing somebody, somewhere. How did they do it?

The answer is simple. Just as Jesus was a man sourced by God, so are all who are filled with His Spirit. Peter explains this in his sermon at Pentecost, where for Christians, it all began. Peter says,

"Men of Israel, listen to this: Jesus of Nazareth was a man accredited by God to you by miracles, wonders and signs, which God did among you through Him, as you yourselves know." (Acts 2:22)

> It is one thing to serve an unrelating god in this world of temptation, heartache, and pain, and another thing entirely to know that Jesus understands my struggles.

Peter tells the crowd of confused onlookers that they should not be surprised at what they are witnessing, for they've seen it before. For what God had done through the man Jesus, He was now doing through them. In short, the identity of the man called Jesus was now the identity of the first Christians.

Even though Jesus was and is God, He became a normal man, just like us. Even though He was born without sin, He was born in a sin-scarred body. Therefore, even though He was not born in a broken relationship with God the Father, His body was just like ours. Jesus aged, got tired, showed emotion, and lived with all the limitations that we as human beings have.

His appetite, for example, was not centered only on the food that was good for him, or did His immune system never falter. Jesus had to learn restraint; as a child He had to learn to walk and be potty-trained, and as an adult He had to allow His sex drive to come under the control and direction of the Holy Spirit.

This fact about Jesus' humanity does not diminish Him as God, but elevates Him to the One who took on humanity, becoming as we are, and yet still overcame. The Bible tells us in Hebrews 2:14-18 that Jesus had to identify with the ones in whom He would save. Since we have flesh and blood and are subject to temptation, He too shared in that weakness. The passage reads,

"Since the children have flesh and blood, He too shared in their humanity so that by His death He might destroy him who holds the power of death – that is, the devil – and free those who all their lives were held in slavery by their fear of death. For surely it is not angels He helps, but Abraham's descendants. For this reason He had to be made like His brothers in every way, in order that He might become a

merciful and faithful high priest in service to God, and that
He might make atonement for the sins of the people.
Because He Himself suffered when He was tempted, He is
able to help those who are being tempted."

This fact about Jesus' humanity does not diminish Him as God, but elevates Him to the One who became human, just as we are, and yet still overcame.

Of course, there is much more the Bible has to teach us about who Jesus became and the reason for His identification with us. However, what we have just discovered, is perhaps enough to show that Jesus' ministry was not just to gift us with salvation, but also to reveal the new identity of those who receive that salvation.

THE CHURCH IN THYATIRA

History, church tradition, and the Bible all contribute to provide valuable information about the city of Thyatira and the church that ministered there.

History tells us the citizens of Thyatira were most likely not aristocrats or politicians, but traders. Ancient ruins reveal that the city boasted of more trade unions than any other city in the Roman empire. From cloth workers and dyers to bakers, slave-traders, and bronze-smiths, the city was rich in commerce and exports. The citizens of Thyatira were, therefore, working-class, blue-collar people.

Church tradition adds to the picture already painted for us by historians. The church in Thyatira was most likely not a very large church. For sure, it never grew to the stature of the church in Ephesus, which was the largest church in the world in that time period. Made up of the traders from the city, it might have looked similar to many of the smaller, working-class churches found throughout the United States today.

As important as history and tradition are, the most valuable insights to the church are found in the Bible. In Revelation 2:18-29, Jesus reveals the spiritual condition of the church. In this small piece of Scripture, we learn that Jesus commended the church for their love and faith, their perseverance and service, and for their growth as a body of believers.

In a time of spiritual poverty, when being a Christian brought social isolation and even, at times, intense persecution, receiving such a commendation would seem to place the church in high spiritual health. Yet Jesus attaches to His commendation a tremendous spiritual rebuke. The church tolerated, even condoned, people living in sin.

Whether it has been commonplace throughout the ages, or ordained for such a time as this, dealing with sin within the church is not easy or popular. Therefore, wherever you live and wherever you attend, you most likely have people in your church living in sin.

After traveling as an itinerant preacher the past two decades, I have visited a lot of churches. I've visited large churches, small churches, churches with great potential, and ones riddled with strife. What I have never come across is "the perfect church."

Because of this, I've had to change my definition of the word *perfect* when it is applied to a church, and ask, "What does the perfect church look like?" Is it the one with no controversy, disagreements, trouble, or arguments? If so, then Jesus' own band of twelve disciples, who made up His church during His earthly ministry, would not qualify to be called *perfect*.

Perhaps the perfect church is not defined by the absence of trouble or problems, but by its identification with Jesus Himself and its willingness to respond to His rebuke. I assure you, if you are looking for a church where the grass is greener and the pews are straighter, you

Whether it has been commonplace throughout the ages, or ordained for such a time as this, dealing with sin within the church is not easy or popular.

will be looking for a very long time. Every church has issues and struggles with controversy; sometimes, if not often times, a church will struggle with its members living in sin.

Without a doubt, sin is a serious and deadly spiritual disease. In order to correctly confront and eradicate sin from the church, sin has to be dealt with and understood Biblically. In the following pages of this book, we will look intently into Jesus' language to the church in Thyatira and discover not only how to deal with sinful people, but learn what sin is, what it is not, and what are the effects of sin in a person's life.

> Without a doubt, sin is a serious and deadly spiritual disease.

KEY CONCEPTS

The key to understanding the Bible is the Bible itself. Although reason, tradition, and experience are great assets to understanding the Bible, the Bible is the most reliable means to understanding God's Word to us.

The only way a person can live a life pleasing to God is to live life empowered by His Spirit.

Jesus demonstrated how to live a life pleasing to God. Whenever we ask, "What Would Jesus Do," we are really asking, "God, will you empower me just like you empowered Jesus."

Sin is not something physical that can be physically cured, but a spiritual condition created by a choice. That spiritual decision creates the physical dilemma.

The *perfect church* is a group of people seeking to live out the Christian life together in patience, forgiveness, and prayer for one another.

REFLECTION QUESTIONS

1. Would you describe your Bible reading more as study time or reading time? Why?

2. What do you do when, while reading the Bible, you come across something you don't understand?

3. Jesus is the example of what a Christian is to look like. We were created in His image and therefore, as He is, we also are to be. For some, this produces guilt. How does this truth make you feel?

4. Read 1 John 3:4-10. What does this passage mean to you?

5. Do you think your church is "perfect?" Explain...

SONS OF GOD

Jezebel

CHAPTER 2

SONS OF GOD

The church in Thyatira is believed to be the smallest of the churches listed in Revelation chapters two and three. Located in close proximity to Pergamum, it was known for its textiles and success in various areas of trade. Unlike the church in Ephesus, the Bible is virtually void of any information about the church. The only reference to Thyatira outside Revelation is found in Acts 16:14, when reference is made of Lydia, "a dealer in purple cloth," who was from the city.

With the rest of the Bible being void of any details about Thyatira, and secular and Church history not offering up much information either, what we can know of the church is limited to the second chapter of Revelation. Yet this small amount of information provides some valuable details which gives some insight into the spiritual condition of the church.

From Jesus' opening statement, we gather that the church in Thyatira is doing many things well.

They have a measure of love and faith, are growing in their service as a body of believers, and are persevering under the persecution that seems so prevalent in that area of the world. Yet alongside this commendation, Jesus gives a strong rebuke to the church: they are tolerating a woman named Jezebel.

As we will discover in the following pages of this book, the label "Jezebel" refers to more than this woman's name, it points to her identity and function in the body of believers. Apart from the title bestowed upon her by Jesus, this woman is known for her authority, her doctrine, and her ability to lead others in the church. Jesus' address to this church centers mainly on this woman and what she represents. As seen in Jesus' concluding remarks, if this church desires to "overcome," then they must confront and expel Jezebel from the body of believers.

CREATED FOR SONSHIP

As we discovered in chapter one, the significance of Jesus' address to each church begins with His approach. Jesus does three things consistently in His approach to each church:

1. Jesus introduces Himself
2. Jesus speaks of the church's context
3. Jesus calls for a result

We also learned that when Jesus introduces Himself, He does so with a description that reveals not only His identity, but also the identity of the church He is addressing. This is to say, that when the church sees who Jesus is, they are also seeing who they are supposed to be. To Thyatira, this description reads:

"These are the words of the Son of God, whose eyes are like blazing fire and whose feet are like burnished bronze." Revelation 2:18

A DIVINE OR HUMAN TITLE?

When I was in college, I survived three semesters of Systematic Theology. One semester focused on God the Father, one on God the Holy Spirit, and one on God the Son. For a year and a half, I studied what the Bible, tradition, and theologians had to say about the Christian, Trinitarian God.

As I have been studying the church in Thyatira, my thoughts have often times drifted back to those classes, and particularly the ones covering Jesus, the Son of God. What I learned in those classes became foundational in how I would view Jesus and myself as children of God.

In calling Jesus *the Son of God*, what often comes to mind is the title declaring His divinity. Jesus is

God, the second member of our triune Christian God. He is of the same substance and is equally God with God the Father and God the Holy Spirit. In my studies of Revelation 2:18, while confronted with Jesus' self-designation, His divinity is what immediately popped into my mind.

Yet this assumption produces a conflict. Those in the church in Thyatira are not divine; they are not God like Jesus is God. If what we have learned thus far in our study of Revelation, namely that Jesus approaches each church to reveal in Himself who they are called to be, then the divine title "Son of God" does not fit Jesus' chosen approach to this church. I mean, how can human beings be divine?

As seen in Jesus' approach, the premise of the Gospel that Revelation proclaims begins with Jesus' identification with the church in their humanity. And He presents Himself as such. Jesus, who is fully God, has become fully human, identifying with humanity in their current fallen state of weakness.[1] This is what makes Him relevant and gives the church hope in their current situation.

> For to say that Jesus overcame the world is one thing, but to say that He overcame as one of us is another thing entirely.

---

[1] Though Jesus was not fallen in nature, having never sinned or being born in sin, He took on a fallen, sin-scarred body.

JESUS, A SON OF MAN, AND ONE OF US

The book of Revelation begins with a lengthy introduction by John. Before presenting what Jesus told him, which was, "to write down and send to the seven churches" (1:11), John introduces four aspects of the prophecy to those seven churches. The first chapter of Revelation is outlined like this:

Verses 1-3   The Prologue
Verses 4-5a   The Persons of God
Verses 5b-8   The Praise to God
Verses 9-20   The Patmos Experience

In the fourth part of his introduction, John describes how he came to the island of Patmos; how Jesus visited him and commissioned him to give the prophecy, and the details of his initial vision of Jesus and the seven churches. John writes of this initial vision in verses 12-16:

"I turned around to see the voice that was speaking to me. And when I turned I saw seven golden lampstands, and among the lampstands was someone like a son of man, dressed in a robe reaching down to his feet and with a golden sash around his chest. The hair on his head was

white like wool, as white as snow, and his eyes were like blazing fire. His feet were like bronze glowing in a furnace, and his voice was like the sound of rushing waters. In his right hand he held seven stars, and coming out of his mouth was a sharp, double-edged sword. His face was like the sun shining in all its brilliance."

In this vivid description of Jesus, there is a particular reference to His humanity in verses 12 and 13, highlighted above. Jesus reveals himself as "a son of man." This phrase is important, for it reveals that John saw Jesus as a human being. This phrase is used consistently throughout the Bible to describe a normal, flesh and blood, human being. There does appear elsewhere a different construction that is translated "the Son of man," that is not what is being communicated here. In this description, John uses language that could be applied to any other man or woman.

This self-revelation is foundational in understanding Jesus' ministry to the church in Thyatira. Jesus is able to minister to Thyatira, because He has identified with Thyatira. He has walked where they have walked, been tempted as they have been tempted, and suffered as they have suffered. You might say that Jesus earned the right to address the church when He became and overcame this world as a human being.

Shortly after I gave my life to Jesus, I began to diligently read the Bible. Of all the stories about Jesus – those showcasing His power and authority, His miraculous healings and feedings, His walking on water, and His supernatural knowledge – what stuck out to me the most, was how human He was.

I have never been an over-achiever. So for me to read that Jesus modeled the life I am supposed to live, was quite intimidating. That is until He proved His humanness. Like me, Jesus got tired (John 4:6), felt frustration (Matthew 17:17-21), showed real emotion (John 2:12-16), and even made mistakes (Luke 2:41-52).

What I encounter when reading through the Gospel accounts of Jesus' life is not a superman type figure living without the natural limitations of every other human being, but a normal, average, everyday man who was filled with the Spirit of God and overcame the world. I agree with Isaiah and think he got it right when he was shown in advance the kind of human being Jesus the Christ would be. Isaiah writes, *"He had no beauty or majesty to attract us to him, nothing in his appearance that we should desire him."* Isaiah 53:2b

If this is not hope then let no person ever speak of hope again, for there is no hope at all. For to say that Jesus overcame the world is one thing, but to say that He overcame as one of us is another thing entirely.

SONS OF GOD. JUST LIKE JESUS

When Jesus addresses the church in Thyatira as a Son of God, He is not differentiating Himself from the church, rather reminding them of their identity as children of God. Whoever receives the Holy Spirit becomes a Christian and walks in relationship to God the Father just as Jesus did. And just as Jesus is the Father's Child, we too are His children. The Apostle Paul goes so far as to say that we can cry out to God calling Him "Dad" or "Daddy." He writes in Romans 8:15,

"For you did not receive a spirit that makes you a slave again to fear, but you received the Spirit of sonship. And by him we cry, "Abba, Father."

To be a Christian is to be God's child and therefore, Jesus' brother.[2] Jesus reminds the church in Thyatira of who they are when He introduces Himself

---

[2] Hebrews 2:5-18

to them. He speaks to them as a sibling would speak to a sibling. They are of the same family, have the same Father, and as children of God, share all the same rights and blessings.

When Jesus speaks to the church in Thyatira as a sibling would speak to a sibling, He is articulating conversationally what humanity's salvation is supposed to look like. As Christians, we have a familiarity with Jesus. We are all children of God.

God's original purpose in creating Adam and his race was that He could have children like His only begotten Son Jesus. We are created in God's image and likeness, and just like Jesus, have a unique relationship with God amongst all of God's creation. Thus human beings were created to be God's kids.

Luke, when penning his Gospel, reserves the last portion of his third chapter to give legal proof of Jesus' claim to be the Messiah. Luke shows that Jesus could trace his family line all the way back to Adam through the family line of David. What is significant about this genealogy in our conversation is who Luke designates as Adam's Father. The last few father-to-son references that lead to Adam reads as follows, *"… the son of Enosh, the son of Seth, the son of Adam, the son of God."* Luke 3:38

As Christians, we have a familiarity with Jesus. We are all children of God.

Adam was God's son. The Bible affirms over and over that God intended for Adam and his race to live in relationship with Him as His children. This is the Good News that not only the Gospel brings, but that Jesus Himself brings to Thyatira.

God created Adam for sonship, but Adam abandoned that relationship when he chose to sin. This choice that Adam made not only affected him, but everyone who would come through him into the world. Humanity, through Adam, abandoned sonship with God the Father.

The Good News of salvation is that Jesus, God's Only Begotten Son[3], has come to bring back the human race into sonship with the Father. And this is salvation: that Jesus took upon Himself the sin of Adam and his race, offering to all who receive Him, His position before the Father as His child.

Jesus' mission was to offer salvation to humanity as well as to show humanity, by His own life, who the Father created them to be. That, of course, is to live with God as our Father just as Jesus does.

---

[3] Jesus' Sonship is different only in that He is the Only Begotten Son, which means He is from the same substance of the Father, fully God, and having never been created. Adam and His race were created for sonship and cannot claim that title by right, but through faith, by grace.

OUR IDENTITY IN CHRIST

It is a staggering reality to embrace that we, who have accepted Jesus as Lord and Savior and received the promised Holy Spirit, are right now God's kids. We are not God's servants or distant relatives, but His children. We are His family. In the Father's eyes, we are just like Jesus.

When God speaks to the church in Thyatira and to you and me, He does so in the same way that He spoke to Jesus. Jesus told His disciples in the hours before His trial and death that whatever we ask of Him, He will grant us. John writes,

"...my Father will give you whatever you ask in my name."
John 16:23

Jesus assures the church in Thyatira, and you and me, that as the Father loves Him, He also loves us. This is because the Father sees us as He sees Jesus. Just as, when we look at Jesus, we see the Father, so also when the Father looks at Jesus, He sees us.

Consider the ramifications of this truth for your life, just as Jesus wanted those in the church at Thyatira to consider it. God has chosen us, among all that He created, to walk with Him in intimacy and oneness. Jesus exemplified this to us and spoke in detail about the kinds of rights and responsibilities we have as God's children.

These are seen also in Jesus' address to Thyatira in Revelation chapter two. Sons of God see with fiery eyes (v.18), walk with legs of burnished bronze (v.18), overcome sin and the world (v.26), and are endowed with the authority that Jesus modeled for us (v.27). These are the blessed gifts that God bestows upon His children.

God wants to bless us! God wants us to overcome the world! God wants us to see with eyes full of revelation and walk the path of His plan for us in victory and prosperity! These are more than simple blessings, they are the rights of every child of God. Yet with these blessings come the responsibilities of embracing this level of living. To live in bondage to sin, defeated by the trials of this world, is to reject who you are in Christ Jesus.

> God has chosen us, among all that He created, to walk with Him in intimacy and oneness.

You were created to overcome as children of the Most High God. Nothing can hinder you. God speaks through the prophet Isaiah saying, "No weapon formed against you shall prevail." (Isaiah 54:17) This means that no strategy, plan, plot, or instrument used to thwart God's plan for you will accomplish its goal. To the church in Philadelphia, Jesus says,

"See, I have placed before you a door that no one can shut. I know that you have little strength, yet you have kept my Word and not denied My name." Revelation 3:8

What an incredible truth! God the Father goes beyond just shielding us as if we were helpless and hopeless servants in a hazardous and treacherous world. He demonstrates in Jesus that His children are mighty conquerers who live in victory and overcome in the paths the Father has laid before them. No door is shut for the child of God who walks in the will and leading of the Holy Spirit.

As we will discover, the rights and responsibilities spoken of to Thyatira, which are echoed throughout God's Word, are not optional for the children of God. They are unavoidably inherent in all who receive the Spirit of sonship. It is my prayer that you embrace your identity and see yourself how God the Father sees you, for it is only here where you will find victory and live the life destined for all children of God.

KEY CONCEPTS

The way Jesus introduces Himself reveals to the church not only who He is, but what they are to look like in their current life situation.

Jesus is the Only Begotten Son of God the Father and the example to every other child of God. God the Father created human beings in the image and likeness of Jesus. He is what a child of God is supposed to look like.

At its core, Christianity is about walking with God exactly as Jesus did.

God created human beings to live in victory and prosperity. God wants us to overcome the world! God wants us to live free of sin and death! God wants us to live lives marked by the supernatural.

REFLECTION QUESTIONS

1. Do you think people today can relate to those in the church of Thyatira? Why or why not?

2. Human beings were created with the ability to "choose." Since Jesus was a human being, He too could "choose." Do you think Jesus could have chosen to sin? Why or why not?

3. When you think of prosperity, what do you think of? Are there any dangers of linking "prosperity" and "Christianity"?

4. Do you think Christians are to live lives marked by supernatural works of God? Have you ever experienced a miracle in your life? If so, what was it?

5. What is the difference between being called "a servant of God" and "a child of God"? Why are children of God often called "servants" in the New Testament? How does Philippians 2:5-11 clarify what it means for a child of God to be a servant?

JEZEBEL

CHAPTER 3

JEZEBEL

It is an exhilarating feeling to sit and write as a child of God. To know that your life has purpose and meaning within the confines of the One and Only True God. That He walks with you and guides you, never leaving you alone, is an overwhelming feeling. He is the Father I've always wanted and the truest of friends. What a blessing it is to be a child of God.

For those who lived and were counted among the body in Thyatira, to be addressed by Jesus as "a child of God" must have been for them what it is for me. Jesus makes no distinction in His address to the church when he speaks of them and Himself. He is one of them and speaks to them as a sibling would speak to a sibling.

Of course, there are differences between Jesus and the Church. Jesus is God (John 1:1-3). Jesus is the First Born over all creation (Colossians 1:15). He is the King of Kings and Lord of Lords (Revelation 17:14), the Messiah (Matthew 1:1), and Savior of humanity (Acts 5:31). He is in Himself, Life (John 14:6), and the Light of the World (John 8:12). He is the Lamb of God who is found to be without spot or blemish (Revelation 5:6) and He is our only hope, for He is Hope (Romans 15:13). In Him all things hold together, for all things were created by Him and for Him (Colossians 1:16-17). He is Jesus of Nazareth and He is both a Son of man (Revelation 1:13) and a Son of God (Revelation 2:18).

The Church is not God, but His body (1 Corinthians 12:27). We are not the first to be born, but are created in His likeness (Genesis 1:26-27). We are His lampstands (Revelation 1:20) and our purpose is to hold up Him, the Lamp (Revelation 21:23), before all people, because He is our Message (Ephesians 3:8). We are dependent upon Him for life (John 14:6) and that life is produced from the Holy Spirit which comes from Him (John 16:7).

When Jesus comes to those in the church at Thyatira and reveals Himself to them, He likens Himself to them - not in role or function - but in identity and position. As children of God, we reign with Him (2 Timothy 2:12) and are seated with Him at the right hand of

We receive, as children, the rights of sons, the same rights that Jesus Himself has as a son.

our Father in Heaven (Ephesians 2:6). We receive, as children, the rights of sons, the same rights that Jesus Himself has as a son (Galatians 4:5). We walk in authority - the authority we have in Him (Revelation 2:26-27) - and we exercise that authority to forgive (John 20:23), encourage and rebuke (Titus 2:15), and build up others in Jesus Himself (2 Corinthians 10:8). Like those in the church at Thyatira, we are the Church and we are children to our Brother (Hebrews 2:10-11), King (John 18:37), and Lord (Revelation 17:14).

JESUS. OUR OLDER BROTHER

This language is important and sets the tone of Jesus' concern for those in Thyatira. In speaking as an older brother to His younger siblings, Jesus rebukes their toleration of a women in their body named Jezebel. His language is aggressive and reveals His shock. The church is tolerating what no one in the family of God should tolerate.

The picture is that of siblings in a back room of a large house. Mom and Dad are in the front room and the kids are speaking together among themselves. The eldest of the kids is distraught and as he speaks, he paces back and forth in front of his dearly loved brothers and sisters. They look at him as those who look at one they also dearly love. They respect him, and as he speaks, they listen closely to his words. "You are tolerating what no one in the family would tolerate!" He says. "How could you tolerate this?"

The Greek word translated "tolerate" literally means "to allow the existence or occurrence of something one dislikes or disagrees with, without interference."[4] It's interesting, Jesus' words give insight to the church. It's not that they agree with what is taking place, but they condone it. They allow this woman called Jezebel to be present and carry on her agendas. This is the issue in the church that Jesus confronts.

JEZEBEL

If you've been around church for any amount of time, you've probably heard of Jezebel. She was a queen of Israel, married to King Ahab in the time of Elijah's prophetic ministry. Ahab and Jezebel mark what some consider the darkest hour of rebellion and sin in Israel's history, save that of the time of Jesus' death.

Insight into this duo is given in the description of Ahab's inauguration as king in 1 Kings 16:29-33:

---

[4] Soanes, C., & Stevenson, A. (2004). *Concise Oxford English Dictionary* (11th ed.). Oxford: Oxford University Press.

"In the thirty-eighth year of Asa king of Judah, Ahab son of Omri became king of Israel, and he reigned in Samaria over Israel twenty-two years. Ahab son of Omri did more evil in the eyes of the Lord than any of those before him. He not only considered it trivial to commit the sins of Jeroboam son of Nebat, but he also married Jezebel daughter of Ethbaal king of the Sidonians, and began to serve Baal and worship him. He set up an altar for Baal in the temple of Baal that he built in Samaria. Ahab also made an Asherah pole and did more to provoke the Lord, the God of Israel, to anger than did all the kings of Israel before him."

There is a tremendous amount of ungodliness and sin that could be detailed about Ahab in the annuls of Biblical history, but surprisingly, it pales in light of his wife and queen, Jezebel.

During king Ahab's reign, Jezebel maintained an immense amount of ungodly influence over him. Through Jezebel, worship of the pagan god Baal entered into Israel. Asherah poles, alters, and temples sprung up throughout the kingdom under her direction. Through her influence, God's own people began to sacrifice their children to pagan gods.

Jezebel was a relentless persecutor of God's prophets. As recorded by the scribe in 1 Kings 18:4, Obadiah hid 100 prophets in caves to protect them from Jezebel's fury. Jezebel's goal was not only to stamp out the teachings of God, but also to remove any trace of His name among His people.

At this time, a famous showdown between Elijah and the false prophets of Baal and Asherah takes place. Preceding the event, Elijah speaks with king Ahab, organizing the details of the duel. In his statements, Elijah reveals who the real spiritual leader of Israel is when he says,

"Now summon the people from all over Israel to meet me on Mount Carmel. And bring the four hundred and fifty prophets of Baal and the four hundred prophets of Asherah, who eat at Jezebel's table." 1 Kings 18:19

When Elijah refers to the false prophets eating at Jezebel's table, he is not referring to Jezebel's responsibilities in the home. Referring to the gathering table as "Jezebel's table" is to assign authority to Jezebel. It was not king Ahab's table, it belonged to Jezebel. She ruled over and directed the activities of the false prophets. And upon their destruction, it was Jezebel who was distraught and who sought revenge upon Elijah. Jezebel was the spiritual leader of Israel during the reign of her husband Ahab.

It was through Jezebel that the persecution of God's prophets and the suppression of His Name took place. Therefore, because of the magnitude of her life of rebellion and hatred of God and His prophets, her name became synonymous with sin.

So when Jesus speaks to the church in Thyatira and refers to a woman named Jezebel, He refers to more than just a woman in their congregation. He assigns to this woman, the history and depravity of what was known in Jezebel. What is more, the spirit at work in this woman was the same spirit that was working in the sinful queen of old.

When Jesus equates sin with Jezebel, He reveals to the church in Thyatira, in a very real and relevant way, the severity of sin. Jesus is not speaking of mistakes when he describes sin; He plucks out of Israel's history a catastrophic result of rebellion and uses that to paint the picture of sin.

> Jesus is not speaking of mistakes when he describes sin. He plucks out of Israels history a catastrophic result of rebellion and uses that to paint the picture of sin.

Jesus' view of sin does not connect with Ahab's consideration of sin, which resulted in his toleration of Jezebel. As revealed by the Son of God, to all children of God, sin is not casual, or is it tolerable in the family of God.

SIN AND MISTAKES

There are two things that must be stated when discussing sin. The first is in regards to the motivation of a sinful action. It seems that often times, in these latter days, sin and mistakes get confused. The husband, having been busted in his pornography use by his wife, responds, "I'm sorry, it was a mistake and it won't happen again!" The young couple, sitting in their pastor's office with their parents, work out the detail of their coming wedding that has resulted from an unexpected pregnancy. Their explanation? "It just kind of happened. We made a mistake."

Maybe these types of explanations come from shame, causing people to distance themselves from the deeds of their own hands, or maybe they are the product of a day and age where courage and character have given way to always playing "the victim." Maybe it's the age-old sinful nature that enslaves mankind to refusing to take ownership of their own actions. Whatever the correct answer may be, all to often there is an attempt to cover up sin by calling it an involuntary, accidental *mistake*.

> As revealed by the Son of God, to all children of God, sin is not casual, nor is it tolerable in the family of God.

Mistakes are not sin and sin is not a mistake. The Oxford English Dictionary defines mistakes and sin very differently. A mistake is defined as,

"Something that is not correct; an inaccuracy"

Sin is defined as,

"An immoral act considered to be a transgression against divine law."

A mistake, then, is an outcome that is inaccurate, but not due to willful disobedience. On the contrary, sin is rebellion. Sin is knowing exactly the "right" and yet choosing the "wrong."

Jesus is very clear on sin, having used Jezebel as an illustration for the church in Thyatira. What is taking place in the church is a rebellion issue, not a mistake issue. Just as Jezebel knew that she was rebelling against the God of Israel, so also this woman among the body of believers must know that she is living in rebellion. After all, Jesus has identified her motives and He is never wrong. He speaks to the church saying,

"Then all the churches will know that I am He who searches hearts and minds..." Revelation 2:23

The second thing that must be stated when discussing sin, is that from a Biblical standpoint, sin is absolutely, utterly, and completely devastating. Sin is never written off as being *casual* or placed in the category of *fluff*.

As a new Christian, I remember struggling through the story of Achan as told in the book of Joshua. Israel has entered the land of promise and under God's direction is taking back what belongs rightfully to them. God directs His people not to take anything from any of the cities, but to destroy everything. So from city to city, the land is reclaimed and no wealth, livestock, or people are plundered.

As chapter 7 opens, Israel is camped outside the city of Ai and they are grieving. They have suffered an embarrassing defeat and as is written,

"...the hearts of the people melted and became like water."
Joshua 7:5

While the people of Israel lose heart, Joshua stands before the Lord learning that sin has found its way into Israel. As the plot unfolds, we learn that a man named Achan had rebelled against God and had taken from Babylonia a robe, two hundred shekels of silver, and a wedge of gold weighing fifty shekels.

Achan did not make a mistake, he rebelled against God.

"Achan replied, 'It is true! I have sinned against the Lord, the God of Israel. This is what I have done..." Joshua 7:20

The result of Achan's sin was devastating, not only for Achan, but for his fellow Israelites and his family. For his sin, Achan was stoned to death. For the people of Israel, they lost the protection and provision of God in battle. For his family, they lost the freedom to live and prosper and suffered the same death that Achan himself received.

My struggle with this story centered on Achan's family. Why should Achan's family suffer Achan's punishment for Achan's sin? What wrong did they do? What sin did they commit? Was it not enough that they suffered, along with the rest of Israel, the defeat of their warriors in battle? What warranted such a severe punishment from God?

The answer is plain not only in this story, but in countless other stories in the Bible. Rebellion against God is so destructive, so perilous, that it not only destroys the person who sins, but also everyone in proximity to them, down to the third and fourth generation.

In this way, sin can be likened to a suicide bomber who not only destroys himself, and not only those in proximity to him, but also those whose context of life is shifted by that individual's action. It is so deadly, in fact, it cannot be overlooked and cannot be dismissed.

Like the suicide bomber, Achan's sin destroyed everyone around him. Like Achan, Jezebel was destroying everyone around her. This is the peril that Jesus comes to address. There is much more at stake than simply a woman's error in leadership. There is sin and destruction exploding in the lives of those who belong to the church at Thyatira.

THE PHYSICAL AND THE SPIRITUAL

As horrific as Achan's story is, when considering the physical ramifications of sin, the spiritual aspect of sin is where the greater horror lies. The physical outcomes that we see and grieve through, are mere consequences and results of the spiritual death exploding in an act of rebellion against God.

It has been my experience that sin is often times defined and discussed in the realm of the physical. The young freshman girl defends her new boyfriend's spirituality by showing his physical church attendance. The husband claims, contrary to his wife's opinion, that he has regular, quality family time; he supports his claim by his physical presence in the home. After the divorce, in an attempt to exonerate herself of the rumor of infidelity, another woman insists she did not have an affair with the man she is currently married to, because they did not physically have sex

> In this way, sin can be likened to a suicide bomber who not only destroys himself, and not only those in proximity to him, but also those whose context of life is shifted by that individuals action.

while she was still married. They only met regularly in secret, held hands, and occasionally kissed.

These are just a few of the many arguments that circulate in the Church today, and though they vary in degree of social acceptance, they all have the common foundation of defining sin in the physical arena of life.

EVERYTHING IS SPIRITUAL

We must never forget and, therefore, be constantly reminded, that everything is spiritual. When God created the first human being, He breathed into his nostrils His very own Spirit and the human being became a living being. Our spiritualness as human beings may be shrouded in this physical tent that we call *a body*, but we are thoroughly spiritual nonetheless.

Consider the gathering of Christians on a Sunday morning. What takes place in a church service is spiritual, and the physical is merely the platform by which the spiritual is expressed. I would contend that you could physically attend church on Sunday morning and yet not spiritually be present. It is the spiritual involvement that transforms singing into worship and giving money into tithe.

As human beings, the war we are born into is spiritual. Our enemy is not flesh and blood, but a spirit. The Bible teaches us,

"For our struggle is not against flesh and blood, but against the rulers, against the authorities, against the powers of this dark world and against the spiritual forces of evil in the heavenly realms." Ephesians 6:12

What is more, the weapons of our warfare are not physical, but spiritual (2 Corinthians 10:3-4).

Human beings are unique in that we engage our world on a spiritual level in physical bodies. As Christians, we are called to walk in this reality and are gifted to do so. The fruit of the Christian life is what is produced by the Spirit. Paul teaches of this spiritual fruit in his addresses to the believers living in Galatia. Paul writes,

"But the fruit of the Spirit is love, joy, peace, patience, kindness, goodness, faithfulness, gentleness and self-control." Galatians 5:22-23

To ignore the spiritual, in light of our physicalness, denies the very essence of who we are as human beings.

SPIRITUAL CONTENT

What makes the book of Revelation so difficult for many students of the Word is this spiritual language. As we've been discovering in our investigation of sin, Jesus speaks to the church in Thyatira about spiritual things, with physical terms, that have spiritual meaning. For example, when Jesus speaks of the woman Jezebel, it is obvious that her name is not Jezebel. Jesus is speaking of a spiritual issue, with the physical term Jezebel, expressing the spiritual problem of sin.

Human beings are unique in that we engage our world on a spiritual level in physical bodies. As Christians, we are called to walk in this reality and are gifted to do so.

This is John's typical writing style in Revelation. To seek to understand Revelation in the realm of the physical leads to confusion and frustration, for the book just doesn't make sense that way.

Jesus does not have a physical sword protruding from His mouth (Revelation 1:16), He does not have glowing eye-sockets (Revelation 2:18), and He has not morphed into a lamb-like animal (Revelation 5:6). The language of Revelation is physically presented to humanity, but spiritual in meaning and interpretation.

This is the crux point for the church in Thyatira. Jesus speaks to the church as an older brother speaks to His fellow brothers and sisters, and His conversation with them is thoroughly spiritual. They are tolerating Jezebel in their body. Who is Jezebel? She is indeed a physical woman in the church, but the name applied to her is spiritual in nature. Jezebel represents sin, and to tolerate her, is to tolerate sin.

There is no dilemma of sin on a spiritual level. Sin, in the spiritual arena of life, is always devastating!

Jesus is grieved over the toleration of Jezebel, for He sees the real damage being done by her, and it is not physical. The cancer of sin is flowing in His body in Thyatira and, therefore, Jesus leaps into action, calling the church to repent.

In the next chapter, we want to look deeper into the spiritual nature of sin, but we can learn a great deal from what we have discovered thus far in Jesus' address to those in the church at Thyatira. Sin is not simply a physical action that is wrong and it is not a mistake or accident. Sin is rebellion against God and it is a spiritual decision that is made. Although sin can at times physically manifest itself in horrific ways, as seen in Achan's life, it often times does not. This is the dilemma of sin on the physical level.

There is no dilemma of sin on a spiritual level. Sin, in the spiritual arena of life, is always devastating! When we sin, we release a cancer that begins producing death. It may not show itself immediately, but it is at work nonetheless. Like a suicide bomber, rebellion produces an explosion that ripples through lives of people, like ripples travel through an entire pond.

The door of rebellion and sin does not lead into the room of the physical, but into the bottomless pit of spiritual death. As we journey further into Jesus' language detailing the consequences of sin, we are going to find that in the DNA of sin, there is an authoritative make-up. To sin is to give away our

God-given authority as a child of God and become a slave.

As we continue investigating Jesus' address to Thyatira, I invite you to prayerfully consider the consequences of tolerating sin.

KEY CONCEPTS

God created human beings in the image and likeness of Jesus. We know this to be true because Jesus is the perfect human being. Therefore, as He is, we are created to be. Jesus is the example of what God intended for humanity.

Mistakes and sin are completely different. Mistakes are accidents and sin is rebellion.

Although sin leaves physical scars, the real impact of sin is in the spiritual realm.

Christians are conduits for the Spirit of God. We bear His fruit and engage our world on a spiritual level. The real battle for the Christian lies in the spiritual, not the physical.

The physical arena of life displays the spiritual consequences of human decision. In this light, our physical life portrays, like a billboard, the condition of our spiritual life.

REFLECTION QUESTIONS

1. What are some things that we "tolerate" in the church today?

2. Based off of what you have learned in this chapter, what is the difference between sin and mistakes?

3. Let's say a man robs a bank. In that act, what is physical and what is spiritual?

4. How does the physical impact the spiritual? Can you give examples from your own life?

5. Why is it wrong to tolerate sin in the body of Christ? Have you ever tolerated sin?

SPIRITUAL AUTHORITY

Jezebel

CHAPTER 4

SPIRITUAL AUTHORITY

"But mark this: There will be terrible times in the last days. People will be lovers of themselves, lovers of money, boastful, proud, abusive, disobedient to their parents, ungrateful, unholy, without love, unforgiving, slanderous, without self-control, brutal, not lovers of the good, treacherous, rash, conceited, lovers of pleasure rather than lovers of God; having a form of godliness but denying its power. Have nothing to do with them." 2 Timothy 3:1-5

In Paul's intimate letter to Timothy, he describes for him a future time when people will be utterly rebellious. The word "rebellion" seems like a fitting word that captures the tenor of all that Paul writes in this statement. The Greek English Lexicon of the NT and Other Early Christian Literature defines rebellion as,

"Independent," "undisciplined," and *"refusing submission to authority."*

Paul describes what kind of people a world apart from Christ will produce.

I believe we are living in the very time in which Paul wrote. We see evidence of this type of character in various genres of music, on college campuses - where students riot for mere entertainment - and in the daily car chases reported on the evening news. We see it portrayed on the movie screen in the willful and rebellious leading man, and on our television screens each evening on the local, national, and world news. Rebellion against authority is all around us, and sometimes, in our local church.

> Anyone who claims to be a child of God will not live a lifestyle characterized by sin and rebellion.

As one who travels the country and preaches in a variety of denominations, I hear much talk about rebellion and sin. I hear many conversations where church goers claim, "we all sin; we all rebel every day in word, thought and deed." In fact, they add, in their misunderstanding of the Word of God, "His grace is sufficient for me."

In the times when I am afforded the opportunity into such conversations, I simply open my Bible to 1 John 3:4-10 and begin to read.

"Everyone who sins breaks the law; in fact, sin is lawlessness. But you know that He appeared so that He might take away our sins. And in Him is no sin. No one who lives in Him keeps on sinning. No one who continues to sin has either seen Him or known Him. Dear children, do not let anyone lead you astray. He who does what is right is righteous, just as He is righteous. He who does what is sinful is of the devil, because the devil has been sinning from the beginning. The reason the Son of God appeared was to destroy the devil's work. No one who is born of God will continue to sin, because God's seed remains in him; he cannot go on sinning, because he has been born of God. This is how we know who the children of God are and who the children of the devil are."

I am admittedly no theologian, but as I already have said, I can read. Anyone who claims to be a child of God will not live a lifestyle characterized by sin and rebellion.

AUTHORITY

As we discovered in the previous chapter, sin is a spiritual decision of rebellion against God. That decision is utterly devastating in not only the life of the one who commits the sin, but in the lives of everyone associated with that decision.

We also found that sin moves beyond the physical into the spiritual core of human existence. This is the focus of Jesus' address to the body of believers in Thyatira. What is more, Jesus seems not to address or seek to correct the physical areas of what is physically produced by sin. What Jesus is concerned about is the spiritual consequences of sin, namely, the issue of authority.

As we noticed in the opening chapter of this book, Jesus' address to the churches is always threefold. He introduces Himself as the example for every Christian, calls the church to look like Him in their context of life, and promises a result in which He alone will bring to pass. It is in this third aspect of His address to Thyatira where we find the real issue He is concerned with regarding sin and humanity. Jesus says,

"To him who overcomes and does my will to the end, I will give authority over the nations — 'He will rule them with an iron scepter; he will dash them to pieces like pottery' — just as I have received authority from my Father." Revelation 2:26-27

The real issue of sin is authority, and we see this is the focus of what Jesus wants to restore to those who make up His body in Thyatira. Jesus identifies a connection between sin and authority when He identifies the result He wants to bring about. Apparently, when sin is tolerated, authority is stripped away.

HUMAN BEINGS

God created humanity to walk in authority. We see this modeled in Jesus, who demonstrated with His life what that authority looks like. He lived a life free of sin, healed the sick, walked on water, and even raised the dead.

Now, before we attribute these expressions of authority singularly to Jesus, we must remember that this miraculous authority was also found consistently among His followers. This authoritative lifestyle started with Jesus and continued on in His body, the Church.

Yet it must be noted that Jesus was not the first human being to demonstrate such right and power. Adam and Eve, the first human beings, were endowed with such authority.

In the first chapter of the first book in the Bible, we read about the creation of heaven and earth. From verses 1 through 25 we learn about the first five days of that creation process and about all that God created on each specific day. Beginning with verse 26 and extending through the end of the chapter, we learn of the creation of the first human beings.

What is most striking about the account detailing the creation of Adam and Eve is the authoritative language that is used. There are words and phrases used, that before that time, were reserved for the description of God alone. Yet when human beings came on the scene, the language was ascribed to them. For example, God says in Genesis 1:26,

"Let us make man in our image, in our likeness...."

This language is unprecedented. In His creative process, God makes humanity unique among all creation. We are one of a kind; the earth, the animals, and even the angels are not like we are. Human beings alone were created in the image of God.

Human beings were also created to rule (Genesis 1:26-28). Before us, God alone ruled. Angels were not created to rule. Animals were not created to rule. Humans, both male and female, were created to rule. On the sixth day of creation, God invited one group of creation to join Him in His rule.

As the remainder of the chapter unfolds, humanity is described with an authoritative language that, once again, before we came along, was language reserved only for God.

Human beings were commanded to "fill the earth and subdue it" (Genesis 1:28). In subduing all the earth, in bringing it under their authority, God placed every seed-bearing plant under humanity's care (Genesis 1:29). In fact, God placed every living creature, "everything that has the breath of life in it," under their authority (Genesis 1:30). In God's creation event, humanity alone was endowed with such authority.

As the first chapter gives way to the second, we read how Adam began walking in that authority. He was placed upon the earth and was instructed to "work and take care of it" (Genesis 2:15). Under God's blessing and in the authority God allotted to him, Adam ministered to the earth.

Adam also named the animals. God did not name them, Adam did (Genesis 2:19-20). And we must understand that Adam did not name the creatures upon the earth in the same manner that some might name their pets. The same word that Adam used when naming Eve, for example, who was his very flesh and blood, he also used in naming the animals. He did nothing flippantly or selfishly, but in the care and wonder of God's perspective, loved and related to his surroundings.

Adam was created in God's "image and likeness." Having the same nature as God, he saw the world and lived in relationship to it, just like God did. All the tenderness and care that God put into His creation flowed similarly through Adam.

These details about Adam paint a clear picture of the authority in which he lived. In a right relationship with God, Adam lived utterly sourced in mind, body, and spirit. Sharing in God's nature, he exercised his authority as a son of God to bring glory to God in all that he did. And all creation benefitted and rejoiced as God spilled through Adam in wonder and beauty.

...AND THEN EVERYTHING CHANGED

"Cursed is the ground because of you; through painful toil you will eat of it all the days of your life. It will produce thorns and thistles for you, and you will eat the plants of the field. By the sweat of your brow you will eat your food, until you return to the ground, since from it you were taken; for dust you are and to dust you will return." Genesis 3:17-19

The picture painted above is quite different than the one painted in chapters one and two. The first picture depicted a scene of a son walking in blessedness, favor, and the authority of his Father. In that scene, not only the son, but all creation benefited from that relationship.

Chapter three paints an entirely different picture. In this scene, the

> Adam was created in Gods "image and likeness." Having the same nature as God, he saw the world and lived in relationship to it, just like God did.

son has rebelled against the Father and eaten from a tree that was forbidden. The consequences of that rebellious act not only affects Adam, but all of creation. Instead of blessings, there are curses. In place of beauty, there are thorns and thistles.

Why so drastic a change? What exactly happened?

Some will tell you that the changes in Adam and Eve, as well as in the world we now live, were a result of the punishment of God for sin. This conclusion neither fits in the context of the passage, nor other places in the Bible where this event is discussed, and grinds against what we know of God's nature and character.

Adam's choice produced the consequences of that choice. In the same way that a child, after being warned by her mother not to touch the stove, burns her hand, so also Adam suffers the consequences of rebelling against God's warning. The pain, hurt, and chaos that follow rebellion against God is not created by God as punishment. Just like the little girl's hand, the effects of sin are the natural consequences of rebellion against God.

FROM SONS TO SLAVES

When Adam sinned, following the logic and advice of Satan over that of his Father and God, he lost his authority as a child of God and became a slave.

Luke's Gospel gives us insight into what really happened when Adam sinned. In Luke 4:1-13, Luke retells Jesus' time of temptation in the wilderness. In this account, Satan leads Jesus to a "high place" and shows Him all the kingdoms of the world. Satan says,

"I will give you all their authority and splendor, for it has been given to me, and I can give it to anyone I want to."

It is clear from what we have already discovered, that God gave Adam authority over all the earth. God gave Adam authority over the animals. God gave Adam authority over all earthly created things. It was Adam who was appointed to rule, not animals, not celestial beings, and certainly not Satan. So how did Satan end up with this authority?

When a human being sins, they do not simply lose or lay aside the authority that is rightfully theirs.

They hand over their authority to Satan and become a slave to his will. In the event commonly called "the Fall," Adam fell from his position of authority over all the earth and in turn, handed that authority to Satan.

This is the real issue of sin. When a person sins, they do not merely do something wrong. They give the enemy authority over what rightly belongs to God's children. Sex, food, entertainment, and all things common to human life become instruments of slavery.

Paul writes to a congregation of believers in Rome about such slavery. He writes,

"Don't you know that when you offer yourselves to someone to obey him as slaves, you are slaves to the one whom you obey--whether you are slaves to sin, which leads to death, or to obedience, which leads to righteousness?"
Romans 6:16

> When a human being sins, they do not simply lose or lay aside the authority that is rightfully theirs. They hand over their authority to Satan and become a slave to his will.

Jesus also speaks of sin and slavery. To the crowd gathering to hear him preach He says,
"I tell you the truth, everyone who sins is a slave to sin."
John 8:34

Sin and slavery go hand in hand, for to sin is to lose the freedom and authority in which humanity was called to live. Yet this slavery is not to the acts of rebellion, but to the very enemy of our soul, Satan, the devil.

ADDICTIONS

The Bible is clear that no one simply quits sinning. No one chooses to stop rebelling against God. The man who, after hearing the convicting message from the pastor, sits in his seat and promises never to look at porn again is kidding himself. The woman who pledges to stop lying, the boy who vows to quit drug use, and the addict who promises to stop abusing alcohol are all examples of well meaning people who do not understand what sin truly is.

You cannot quit sinning. You must be delivered from the control and exploit-ation of the enemy. This is where deliverance is found. The problem is not in the sex drive, the alcohol, the tobacco, or the anger. The stronghold is found in the past, where Satan was given authority in a specific area of your life. As my mammy would say, "never give the enemy a foothold in your life."

> The Bible is clear that no one simply quits sinning. No one chooses to stop rebelling against God.

Mammy is right. He's not after the "bad" action, he seeks to control and destroy us through the choices we make. And when we make the choice to turn from what we know to be God's direction and will, in that moment of time, we are handing authority over to Satan to do as he pleases in that area of our life. This is precisely where we find the root of addiction and slavery.

I was a smoker from my early teen years through my early twenties. Although I don't endorse smoking (I mean...it causes cancer) I don't encourage quitting for the same reason that some Christians might. My problem with smoking comes back to the slavery issue.

As a smoker, I was dependent upon cigarettes. They calmed my nerves, eased my boredom and gave me an identity that, for a variety of reasons, I liked. For me, smoking was more than just smoking. The cigarette was the companion and ally that I could always count on.

When Jesus came into my life and I began to live life with Him, I began to see two specific things about my smoking habit. The first was that my old companion resembled more of a slave-master than an ally, more of a crutch than a support. The second was the cigarette stood in the place where Jesus was supposed to stand.

And so I was delivered from smoking. Quitting was hard. The physical addiction was challenging to overcome, for sure, but the psychological and emotional addiction was equally as difficult. But as I released the dependence on smoking to Jesus, He replaced it with reliance and strength found only in Him. I have been free, truly free, of the dependence on smoking for over 17 years.

THE OPPORTUNITY FOR SIN

The Bible reveals that Satan is not only a liar, but "the father of all lies." When he lies, he speaks his native language. In regards to sin, the lie is that the rebellious act is only an action. Satan would have us believe he is interested in us performing wrong actions, doing wrong things. The truth is, those actions are merely vehicles for him to gain authority in our lives.

Satan does not want us just to do bad things anymore than God just wants us to do good things. Our enemy wants to gain authority in our life. Both God and Satan want authority in our life; this is the fundamental struggle of human spirituality.

An opportunity for me to sin surfaced shortly after my wife and I purchased our first home. For the first eleven years of our marriage, we lived on the road in a motorhome. In between revivals and camps, we would stay with various friends or family. But in 2009 we struck camp and secured a place of our own in Watertown, Tennessee.

Having a house required us to have another vehicle. We had the motorhome and a jeep to pull behind it, but we found we also needed a second vehicle at the house for when I was on the road and Karenda was left at home. After a lot of searching and even more praying, we found a 1999 Ford Explorer Eddie Bauer edition.

The price was perfect and we agreed to pick up the SUV on our next trip to Indiana. I had kept my neighbor informed of our need for a car and after we found the Ford, I let him know the good news. What he brought to my attention made the good news a little less good.

> Both God and Satan want authority in our life: this is the fundamental struggle of human spirituality.

We had saved and scrapped together $3,000 for a vehicle and we didn't have a penny more. What I had not calculated into my budget, as my neighbor clearly pointed out, was the cost for registration and plating the vehicle. Over the years I had purchased several vehicles, but they were always in the name of the ministry and were not subject to the kind of taxes that a personal vehicle was subject to. I was devastated when I realized I would have to scrape together another $400 to make the vehicle legal.

It was in this moment, when despair was setting in, that my neighbor offered a ray of hope. He looked at me and said, "Ya know, there's a way around paying that $400. When you pick up the car, give them the $3,000 and sign the title, but instead of putting down that you paid $3,000, put down that you paid $300. You'll pay tax on the $300 instead of the $3,000 and save your $400." He then added, "And if the seller has a problem with that, bribe them with 50 bucks, you'll still come out ahead."

My first thought, after doing the math in my head, was that he was a genius! But my second thought came shortly after, and from the Lord. What was suggested was not only dishonest, but was stealing from the government.

I thanked my friend for his advice, shook his hand, and while turing to walk back across the yard to my house, made the decision about what I would do. I would pay the $3,000 for the Ford, write on the title that I payed $3,000, and pony up the $400 for registration and plates.

The cost of lying and stealing was too great a price to pay, for the real price would not be dollars and cents, but the loss of God's blessing and authority in my personal finances. If I would have buckled to the advice of my friend and saved the money that I did not have, I would have opened the door for Satan to come in and have authority in my personal finances. I would have taken the control of how I spend money, what I do with money, and my perspective of money and put it in the hands of the enemy of my soul.

I look back at that decision now and then and praise God I did not relent to the temptation that seemed so great at the time. The cost would have been more than I could have ever paid, for like Adam, it would have spread from me, to my wife, to my children and into every financial transaction I would ever make.

Satan did not want me to just steal or lie about money. He wanted authority in that area of my life. He wanted every financial transaction from that point forward under his direction and control. Praise God that he does not have that control in my life. Praise God that I am not a slave to money.

I often wonder, while I'm writing, what you, the reader, are thinking about what I am sharing. I wonder if you have sinned or are living in rebellion and are now realizing who is at work in your life. If you need a sign, there are always clues to bondage and slavery. Do you have an area of your life where you consistently fall? Is there something in your life that always gets the better of you? More than likely, this is an area where, at some point, you have allowed the enemy to have control.

There is hope for you in Jesus. You do not have to live as a slave to Satan! You can be free! It is possible to overcome! But you need to confess what you have done, realizing that it was more than an error in judgement or mistake in action, and ask Jesus to remove the hands of the enemy from your life. Ask God to free you from bondage and slavery in that area of your life.

Remember, Satan lied to you at some point and did not tell you what he was really after. Confess this to God, for He already knows it completely. Ask Him to free you and to come in and reside where the enemy once staked his claim. Then no longer give yourself over to that lie which once enslaved you, but respond to the voice of Jesus Christ when temptation returns.

I pray that you will overcome and experience life as a free and authoritative child of God. Lord Jesus, let it be so in our life.

KEY CONCEPTS

Anyone who claims to be a child of God will not live a lifestyle characterized by sin and rebellion.

Adam was created in God's "image and likeness." Having the same nature as God, he saw the world and lived in relationship to it, just like God did. This is also what God desires for you.

When a human being sins, they do not simply lose or lay aside the authority that is rightfully theirs. They hand over their authority to Satan and become a slave to his will. Remember: Sin = Slavery.

The Bible is clear that no one simply quits sinning. No one chooses to stop rebelling against God.

REFLECTION QUESTIONS

1. How do you define rebellion?

2. Do you think rebellion is a good word to describe sin? Why or why not? If not, what word would you use?

3. What are some consequences of Adam & Eve's sin?

4. Discuss the error in this phrase: "I'm not hurting anyone but myself."

5. How do we lose the authority that God gives us?

6. Do you struggle with addiction? Confess it by saying it out loud. What are you going to do about that addiction?

JEZEBEL'S CHILDREN

CHAPTER 5

JEZEBEL'S CHILDREN

My father died in 1999. I am a lot like my dad. My temperament, being organized, and a stickler for finances are all attributes that somehow trickled down to me. But these similarities are just personality. There are also the physical similarities. At his funeral, I saw his sister, my aunt, whom I hadn't seen since I was a little boy. When she saw me, she threw her hand up to her mouth, rocked back on her heals, and stared in shock. I remember her saying, "You look just like Joe."

I am not my father. I may look like him and in some ways, act like him, but I am thoroughly *Jeremiah*. There is only one of me that walks the face of this earth. I have a call upon my life and was created by God for that purpose. Before I was born, He knew me and fashioned me for His plan and pleasure. Yet still, there is the family resemblance. I suppose this is how it has always been with sons and their fathers. Our DNA, in one way or another, bears us out.

It is important to see humanity in this way. We bear the image of our human fathers, but we also bear – if we are spirit-filled Christians – the image of our Father in Heaven. Remember, human beings are unique among all the creatures under heaven, for we were created to be children of God. Therefore, when we become who God desired us to be through faith in Jesus Christ, God becomes our Heavenly Father and we become His child.

I've pondered whether I am theologically accurate when I write that we were created "to be children of God" rather than created "as children of God." It seems clear, to propose the latter would take away choice. Human beings were created with what theologians call *free will*.

I suppose in one sense, all human beings are children of God. Humanity, by God's design, is so thoroughly wrought with choice and freedom that even though God will always be our Creator, He may not always be our Father. From what we read in Scripture, Fatherhood, in the spiritual sense, depends on choice and not on right.

CHILDREN OF GOD

When Jesus speaks to the body of believers in Thyatira, He addresses them in light of the choice they have made to receive the Good News of Salvation. To be a Christian is to believe who Jesus claimed to be and to receive from Him, by our own choosing, the right to become children of God. This is how John describes salvation to his readers when he pens the prologue to his Gospel. He writes,

"Yet to all who received Him, to those who believed in His Name, He gave the right to become Children of God; children born not of natural descent, nor of human decision or a husband's will, but born of God." John 1:12-13

The choice in salvation is the choice of belief. To believe Jesus is to embrace God not only as the Father of Jesus, but also as our own Father. In that choice, we who have believed are filled with the Spirit of Jesus and walk with the Father just as Jesus did. We bear the name *child*, just as Jesus does, and we receive all the benefits and blessings that are in Christ. This is what makes the issue in Thyatira all the more disastrous. What is at stake is the choice of a Father.

> Humanity, by Gods design, is so thoroughly wrought with choice and freedom that even though God will always be our Creator, He may not always be our Father.

It is important to note in Jesus' address, how He refers to those who have come under the authority of Jezebel. He does not call them "students," nor does He call them "disciples;" Jesus calls them her "children."

As we have already discovered, the relationship God chooses to have with us is that of a parent-child relationship. God is not our boss or our master, but the Father who teaches, looks after, protects, and blesses His children.

What sometimes is overlooked, however, is that Satan also desires to be a father. His fathering, of course, does not look anything like the fathering of God, but it is still fathering nonetheless. As Jesus reveals in the relationship between Jezebel and her children, whenever the discussion of sin and human beings begin, Satan as a father must be included in the conversation.

This language sheds new light on the consequences of sin in a person's life. As we have already learned, by Adam's example, when a person sins, that person opens themselves up to Satan and his authority in their life. What we are concerned with in this chapter, considering this new language used by Jesus, is the type of authority that we give Satan if we do sin.

TYPES OF AUTHORITY

We live in a world filled with authority. I remember as a teenager looking forward to the day when I would move out of my mom's house and into a place of my own. Then I could do whatever I wanted! I could stay up late, go to bed whenever I chose, sleep in as late as I wanted, clean when I wanted, eat what I wanted whenever I wanted and so on and so on. It isn't hard to believe, that life on my own was a rude awakening from the dream I thought it would be.

Instead of being released from all authority, I found the opposite to be the reality. From my landlord to my roommate, I was in the same boat. My boss at work, the policeman in his squad car, and even my own unleashed lusts seemed to exert their authority over my life. The delusion of living free of authority quickly disappeared.

In my life I find a variety of authorities which call me into account. There is the local authority which decides how fast I can drive, when and where I have to stop and go, and where I can travel and where I am confined. There is the authority of the church in which I minister. That authority holds me accountable to the message I am called to preach, the lifestyle I maintain outside of the pulpit and even the kinds of food and beverages I put into my body. Even my wife has authority in my life. As the other half of my body, she has authority over my time, my entertainment and my bodily drives.

Authority is an unavoidable part of life. We experience it as people under authority and as people who possess authority over others. Yet for the person who maintains a Biblical perspective of sin, there is a specific distinction among types of authority.

There are two areas of spiritual authority. There is the authority found in a right relationship with God and there is the authority found in a life of sin and rebellion. Both areas of authority manifest in the parent-child relationship.

As seen in Jesus' description of Jezebel and her children, those who fall under the control of the enemy, become more than students. They become children. Satan exerts a parental authority over those whom he enslaves. He is not a dictator-type figure who commands from a distance what will and will not be done, but a father-figure who mentors and trains his children.

While watching the evening news a few months ago, my wife and I learned that a child predator in our town had just been captured. We literally felt sick as the news anchor described what the man was accused of. I remember perfectly the look on my wife's face when she looked at me and asked, "How could a person do that to a child?"

This answer, in light of what we are learning about sin, is simple. The man did not have to force himself to abuse the child. He found pleasure in what he was doing. He did not see the child the way you or I would, but saw through the eyes of his spiritual father.

At some point in his past, this man rebelled against God and allowed the enemy to have authority in his life. Satan seized this authority and began to mentor, shape and twist him into the type of man he eventually became. The consequences of sin were obvious to my wife and me; we witnessed them that night on the evening news.

The horrific acts that men and women inflict upon one another in this world, as shocking and repulsive as they are, begin to make sense when the effects of sin are considered.

POIEO

Jesus often spoke about sin during His earthly ministry, for it was the central issue and purpose of His life in this world. Jesus came to remove sin from the human equation. This is exactly how an angel described Jesus after Joseph learned Mary was pregnant. The angel says,

"She will give birth to a son, and you are to give Him the name Jesus, because He will save His people from their sins." Matthew 1:21

In Jesus' teachings, He was specific about His ministry. Jesus taught that the real problem with sin is not in wrong actions, but that those actions spill out of the kind of people we are. From the moment of rebellion, a person embraces the same choice that Adam made in his rebellion, which puts Satan in place of God as father. With the enemy as our father, we have no chance of living a life pleasing to God.

Jesus uses a variety of stories and language to describe this to us. One word in particular sheds light on the parent-child consequences of sin and continually pops up in Jesus' teachings.

The Greek word *poieo*, translated "do, doing, done, and does" in most English translations of the Bible, describes both what Jesus does as a Child of God and what sinful men do as children of the devil.

> With the enemy as our father, we have no chance of living a life pleasing to God.

116

Poieo is an interesting word for describing something that is done. In other books written in Jesus' day, the Greek word poieo describes how trees produce fruit. I don't know about you, but I don't use the word *do* when describing how trees produce fruit. A tree *bears* fruit, it *produces* fruit, but it doesn't *do* fruit.

In its due season, depending on what kind of tree it is, that's the type of fruit it will produce. Thus, we know the difference between an apple tree and a pear tree. Apple trees and pear trees produce different kinds of fruit because they are different kinds of trees. It's that simple.

This is the thought behind the word poieo. There are a few other words Jesus used when describing what He did and did not do, all of which can be translated do, but Jesus chose this word to explain His actions over against the actions of sinful men. Its meaning is specific and Jesus chose the word for that meaning.

Just as an apple tree *does* apples, Jesus *did* what was consistent with who He was as a child of God, and sinful men *do* what is consistent with being children of the devil. This is why Jesus used illustrations about trees and their fruit regularly in His preaching ministry.

In His Sermon on the Mount, Jesus uses *fruit* language to describe how to distinguish sinful men from Godly men. Jesus says,

"Watch out for false prophets. They come to you in sheep's clothing, but inwardly they are ferocious wolves. By their fruit you will recognize them. Do people pick grapes from thorn bushes, or figs from thistles?" Matthew 7:15-16

Apparently, identifying the righteous from the unrighteous is just like distinguishing an apple tree from a peach tree. You simply look at the fruit.

John records in his Gospel a conversation between Jesus and a group of Israel's leaders about this very issue. Jesus claims that God is His Father and they claim Abraham is theirs. It is almost comical to hear Jesus' response to their claims. Jesus says,

"If you were Abraham's children, then you would do (poieo) the things that Abraham did. As it is, you are determined to kill me, a man who has told you the truth that I heard from God. Abraham did not do (poieo) such things." John 8:39-40

It is absurd to suggest that from Jesus' perspective, they are Abraham's children. For what was going on inside of Abraham, making him do what he did, was not going on inside of them. Jesus adds,

"You are doing (poieo) the things your own father does (poieo)." John 8:41

The leaders of Israel do have a father, and are doing the things that their father does, but that father is not Abraham. As the conversation continues, Jesus tells them,

"You belong to your father, the devil, and you want to carry out your father's desires." John 8:44

The conversation is heated, as it always is when sin is being discussed, and Jesus gives us crystal clear insight into these men and why they operate the way they do. The actions of this group of Jews line up perfectly with the actions of the devil. The reason they are trying to kill Jesus is because Satan also wants to kill Jesus. They are following in the path of the one who had fathered them.

> In Jesus, we see more perfectly than ever before, what God looks like and how He feels.

Jesus, on the other hand, is altogether different. His actions line up perfectly with those of God

Himself. What is more, the early church, the first disciples, and Apostles proclaim that in the person of Jesus we see for the first time who God really is! In Jesus, we see more perfectly than ever before, what God looks like and how He feels.

GOD OUR FATHER

As we've already seen in earlier chapters of this book, some Christians get confused when they think about sin. This confusion is not accidental. It is Satan's ploy to deceive humanity. It is how he deceived Adam and Eve and it is how he spiritually attacks you and me. If Satan can distract us from the real issue, leading us to believe sin is only an act, then he can gain control in our life. He can capture and enslave us to his will. Remember, he does not want people to boss around, he wants men and women to think, act, and live with his perspective.

Although I never really read the Bible as a child, I did attend church fairly regularly. Whether it was my lack of understanding or my inability to keep awake, I never understood what it meant to be a Christian. Oh, I believed the surface level stuff, that there was only one God and that Jesus was the Savior of the world. I believed this with all my heart. What I didn't grasp, was the deeper and real Truth that Jesus came to make us like Himself.

I believed, all the way up to the day I was saved, that Jesus wanted to save me from going to Hell. I thought that's what the whole *Christian deal* was about. Jesus wanted me to go to Heaven and live in bliss, not go to Hell and live with blisters.

Yet I believed there was a barrier, a blockade to His salvation. That barrier, of course, was me. The only way He could save me, I thought, was for me to quit doing bad things and start doing good things. I had no idea that the bad things I was doing were actually permission-giving-choices enabling the enemy to come into my life and father me.

Throughout my teen years and early twenties, I would lie in bed at night and pray that Jesus would not let me die in my sleep. I remember praying that I believed in Him and wanted to go to Heaven, but that I wanted to have fun for a while. I wanted to drink and do drugs. I wanted to have sex and live crazy. I was still young and wanted to live it up for a while! I wanted Jesus to protect me during those years, because I did believe in Him. Then, when I was old and decrepit and unable to have

> Jesus wanted me to go to Heaven and live in bliss, not go to Hell and live with blisters.

fun anymore, I would line up to His rules and live responsibly as He desired. Then He would save me and I would go to Heaven.

Isn't that sad? It's embarrassing actually. Only now do I realize the real consequences of my actions. Jesus did not come to save me from doing bad things. Jesus came to deliver me from the one I allowed to enslave and father me.

All those years of living for the moment were years spent being fathered by Satan. I had allowed him to teach me about all kinds of things, not least how to handle money, how to look at women, and how to fulfill my bodily drives.

Of course, when Jesus entered my life, He not only forgave and forgot my sin, but began to transform the way I thought. Paul teaches about this work when writing to the church in Rome. In Romans 12:1-2 Paul writes,

"Therefore, I urge you, brothers, in the view of God's mercy, to offer your bodies as living sacrifices, holy and pleasing to

> Sin is not as much theological as it is personal. The affects of sin are never felt in the classroom, but in the day-to-day routines of life. Bondage and slavery are personal torments, not theological exercises.

God - this is your spiritual act of worship. Do not conform any longer to the pattern of this world, but be transformed by the renewing of your mind."

There is hope of forgiveness of sin and for a life lived in rebellion against God. Jesus is that hope, for He alone can save us. However, there are also patterns of behavior and a warping of the mind that does not simply disappear the moment Jesus comes to live in our life. This is the price tag of sin and it is costly indeed.

IT'S A PERSONAL THING...

Sin is not as much theological as it is personal. I mean, the affects of sin are never felt in the classroom, they are felt in the day-to-day routines of life. Bondage and slavery are personal torments, not theological exercises.

Let me be honest with you. From the moment Jesus became Lord of my life, I tried not to sin. I would like to be able to tell you that after I became a Christian, I never sinned. This, unfortunately, is not the case. There were times when I simply wanted my will over His.

Yet as I grew in my relationship with Jesus, understanding more about Him and how good He really is, I rebelled against Him less. But when He revealed to me through the Bible, the truth about sin and the devastating bondage it would cause in my life, I chose to never rebel against Him again. The consequences were just too great.

There is no room for sin in the life of a child of God, for the consequences are not physical, but spiritual. The Bible is plain about this. John teaches in his first epistle the Christian stance on sin. He writes,

"Everyone who sins breaks the law; in fact, sin is lawlessness. But you know that He appeared so that He might take away our sins. And in Him is no sin. No one who lives in Him keeps on sinning. No one who continues to sin has either seen Him or known Him. Dear children, do not let anyone lead you astray. He who does what is right is righteous, just as He is righteous. He who does what is sinful is of the devil, because the devil has been sinning from the beginning. The reason the Son of God appeared was to destroy the devil's work. No one who is born of God will continue to sin, because God's seed remains in him; he cannot go on sinning, because he has been born of God. This is how we know who the children of God are and who the children of the devil are: Anyone who does not do what is right is not a child of God; nor is anyone who does not love his brother." 1 John 3:4-10

CONSIDERATIONS

I would like to ask you to consider two things as we come to the close of this chapter. First, where are you allowing the enemy of your soul to have authority in your life? Where are you giving him permission to teach, train, and father you? Consider carefully what these choices mean for you and your family.

Lastly, where are you living in constant defeat? I tell you the truth, you were never intended to live a life of defeat! The Bible teaches that we are overcomers, even more than conquerers in Jesus Christ. If you are living in bondage, ask the Lord to release you from the hand of the enemy. Confess the choice that allowed Satan to gain authority over you and ask Jesus to take His rightful place in that area of your life.

As Christians, we must live out the remainder of our lives being fathered by God! He will constantly reveal patterns of behavior and ways of thinking that were not produced by Him. Confess these and ask Him to shape your heart and mind to flow in synchronization and obedience to His will. He will do it! He wants to do it! It is His plan of salvation.

KEY CONCEPTS

Choice is a fundamental part of being human.

Anyone who lives in a consistent pattern of rebellion and sin cannot please God.

The things we do in our day-to-day life spill out of the spiritual condition of our soul.

God does not want to be our Boss, Supervisor, or Consultant: He wants to be our Father. God desires for us to live in the parent-child relationship with Him.

You can live free from sin!

REFLECTION QUESTIONS

1. What makes us unique among all the creatures under heaven?

2. What choice do we make in salvation? How do we actually become a child of God?

3. Why is it important that we are called *children of God* instead of *servants* or *slaves*?

4. Define the word *poieo*. Does this word change the way you understand your actions?

5. How does the idea of *poieo* relate to whom we've chosen to be our father?

6. Do you believe that a child of God sins? Why or why not? Explain.

GOD'S PLAN TO FATHER

Jezebel

CHAPTER 6

GOD'S PLAN TO FATHER

I tell people all the time that I was born to be a dad. Now, whether we admit it or not, there are downsides to having children. Your Friday nights, finances, and emotional well being all change when you have children. But I can testify, the upsides far outweigh the downsides!

There's just something about having your four-year-old stumble into your bedroom at 6am to snuggle up beside you and fall back to sleep. There's no greater joy than hearing "dad" or "mom" for the first time, especially when it's your child saying it. Watching your child take their first steps, encouraging them as they pull their first tooth, and listening to them read their first book are all privileges that only a parent can appreciate.

Then there's the mentoring, shaping, and teaching your child. As one who works primarily from home, I get to spend enormous amounts of time with my kids. Whether it's playing disc golf or combing "Tangled's" hair (you know, Disney's version of Rapunzel), I have been blessed with the opportunity of experiencing these adventures personally with my kids.

COMPARISONS

The Bible often compares God's parenting with our parenting. It's a fitting illustration. We were created in His image and likeness and, therefore, can relate to God, however minutely, in how parents feel about their children. In His Sermon on the Mount, Jesus speaks to the crowd saying,

> The truth is, God enjoys being our Father. It was the motivation behind His creating us.

"If you, then, though you are evil, know how to give good gifts to your children, how much more will your Father in Heaven give good gifts to those who ask Him?" Matthew 7:11

The truth is, God enjoys being our Father. It was the motivation behind His creating us.

As I've already written, over the last couple years, I have given considerable time to studying through the book of Revelation. My study of the church in Laodicea, and specifically Jesus' introduction of Himself, sheds tremendous light on our identity as children of God.

Jesus introduces Himself to Laodicea as the "Beginning of God's creation" (Revelation 3:14 ESV). It is a marvelous comparison of Jesus and the church.

The Greek word translated beginning is the same word used in John 1:1, when John writes, "In the beginning...", and the same word used in Genesis 1:1, in the Greek translation of the Old Testament, when Moses writes, "In the beginning..."

These *beginnings* are one and the same and do not refer to time, but to Jesus. Jesus tells the church in Laodicea that He is that *beginning*. Think about it. When God looked at Jesus, His only begotten Son, an overwhelming love and passion stirred within Him to have other children just like Jesus.

So, the creation event recorded for us in Genesis spilled forth. God created the world and everything in it out of His longing for more of Jesus. The universe – as vast and incomprehensibly intricate as it is – was

> When God looked at Jesus, His only begotten Son, an overwhelming love and passion stirred within Him to have other children, just like Jesus.

created to be the setting where God could live, love, and father His children.

A SINFUL BOTCHING

This entire book has centered on the problem of sin. Not sinful activities or sinful behavior, but the root of sin. In the words of my generation, "Sin jacked everything up." God's entire plan, His only begotten Son, His entire created family, all the heavenly beings, and all that is known and unknown in space and time shook and changed because of Adam's sin.

Adam did not merely eat of a tree that was forbidden to him, he walked out of the family of God. Knowing he made a choice outside the character of the Only Begotten Son, and yet being deceived as to the extent of what that choice would produce, Adam rebelled against his Dad. He rebelled against his *Abba*.

The story unfolds throughout the pages of Scripture of how God relentlessly pursued His children. Jesus gives a beautiful depiction of God's heart in the story of *The Prodigal Son*. The father in that story does not write-off his son, but waits in expectation for him to return to the family.

Of course, there are other stories which shed more light on the matter. God has not sat on His Heavenly porch waiting for us to come home, He has initiated our return. He invented a way to save us!

Our Heavenly Father has crossed every threshold, leapt every chasm, and moved every mountain to reach, persuade, and redeem His beloved children. He sees our plight and seeks to save us from the Hell that awaits us. That is, *Hell* being the only fitting word to describe life without God as a Father. Jesus, our older brother, said it perfectly,

"For God so loved the world that He gave His One and Only Son, that whoever believes in Him shall not perish but have eternal life. For God did not send His Son into the world to condemn the world, but to save the world through Him. Whoever believes in Him is not condemned, but whoever does not believe stands condemned already because He has not believed in the name of God's One and Only Son." John 3:16-18

The real situation of humanity is that we are all lost, each and every one of us. We are headed to a place, by our own choosing, where men and women are estranged from God eternally. Therefore, God acts! He intervenes! He comes to us in the person of Jesus, our older Brother, and calls us back.

It is a fantastic picture! Jesus tells us that God is putting it all behind Him and forgiving us. In Jesus' death on the cross, Satan's leverage is destroyed! It's taken away. It is no more! All we have to do is believe. We have to believe in Jesus.

We have to embrace God through Faith in Jesus, which means we accept what God has accomplished through His Son, choose to be filled with the Spirit of His Son, and live lives characterized by the Life of His Son. In turn, we are transformed, regenerated, and renewed once again into the likeness of His Son.

So much so, that when God looks at Jesus, He sees us. And when we look at Jesus, we see the Father. Jesus is the *crux* of salvation, the Way, the Truth, and the Life for all who would be saved. In Jesus, we at last can be reconciled to God as His children, and He to us as our Father.

THE LANGUAGE OF A FATHER

Even though I grew up estranged from my dad, God has blessed me over the years with several father-figures. If you've grown up not having your dad involved in your life, you may be able to identify with me. Whether a neighbor, teacher or grandparent, God always seems to place in our life the right man, at the right place, at the right time.

My wife and I had a very difficult time early on in our marriage. If there was ever a time I needed the guidance of a father, it was during those early years. It was during that tumultuous season of marriage that God brought Stephen Manley into my life.

I looked up to Stephen. Back in college I had travelled for a summer with him as an intern. I listened to him preach, watched him interact with people, and witnessed how he lived out the message of the Gospel in his day-to-day life. Needless to say, whenever he offered me advice, I took it.

> Jesus is the crux of salvation, the Way, the Truth, and the Life for all who would be saved. In Jesus, we at last can be reconciled to God as His children, and He to us as our Father.

One afternoon, during our annual Cross Style Training Camp, he asked if he could talk with me in private. Of course I agreed and we went back to his motorhome to chat. He told me how much he believed in me and that I even reminded him of himself when he was my age.

I was elated! Wow! What a compliment! Then he added, "If you don't make some changes in your life, your wife is going to end up leaving you."

I went from soaring in the clouds to crashing in the sea. I was crushed, shocked, and dumbfounded all at the same time! I remember sitting there just staring at him. What was he saying? What did he mean?

Our time together that afternoon was long and uncomfortable for both of us, but it was a much needed conversation. Looking back, what he told me probably saved my marriage. As a father would have, Stephen helped me see that I was putting ministry before my responsibilities as a husband. "Put your wife first," he said. So I did, and Karenda and I are still growing and learning how to minister together till this day.

> God wove clues within the fabric of His creation, waiting to be discovered, that reveal the kind of intimacy He desires to share with us.

Whether it is your own father or a father-figure, having a godly man around to give fatherly advice is crucial in the Christian life. Now, some might think this is true merely due to the life experience of a father-figure. Yes, this is probably true, but misses the point I'm trying to make.

God's design for fathers and their children is to give us insight into how He desires to relate to us. Remember the Matthew 7:11 quote we looked at just a few pages ago? "...how much more will your Father in Heaven..." God's creative design is not random, but filled with intention. God wove clues within the fabric of His creation, waiting to be discovered, that reveal the kind of intimacy He desires to share with us.

All of the godly men who have served as father-figures in my life were being used by the Holy Spirit not to just give me good advice and sound teaching, which is certainly true, but to be the physical demonstration of the spiritual role my Heavenly Father was playing in my life. God was at work in those men. It was my Heavenly Father who was instigating those conversations.

I've often wondered how all those details fit together. At what times were men speaking to me on their own and what times were they being used by God. It seems kind of risky to look at father-figures this way. Maybe it is enough, in regards to our conversation, to listen to the words of Jesus in John 10:14-15a on this matter:

"I am the good shepherd; I know my sheep and my sheep know me-just as the Father knows me and I know the Father."

Perhaps it is enough to trust God with the risk of following a voice that is not His. I trust that He will speak in a way that I can hear and with such clarity that I will be able to distinguish His Words from all others.

EYES LIKE BLAZING FIRE

The language that Jesus uses when speaking to Thyatira is language delivered through Jesus from our Heavenly Father. When Jesus speaks, He does so from His identity as a child of His Father. He sees Himself through His Father's eyes.

This is extremely important for you and I, for we are to recognize in Jesus how we are to identify ourselves. God desires for us to see ourselves through His eyes. All too often we believe what others say about us or see ourselves through someone else's eyes. The enemy uses this tactic against us all the time.

If you've ever felt, or even heard in your mind, that you are worthless, dumb, dirty, or any other description that is not consistent with what the Bible teaches about children of God, recognize that those feelings or that voice is not from your Father in Heaven. He does not see you that way and, therefore, does not talk to you that way! That voice is from your adversary, the devil. It is a lie, so name it as such and declare out loud that you are a *blessed*, *wonderful*, and *privileged* child of God.

When Jesus describes Himself as having fiery eyes, He is indeed drawing upon how God the Father sees Him, but He also chooses this language to describe how God desires to father His children.

Knowing what we have already discovered, that much of the language used in Revelation is plucked out of the Old Testament, when we look at the word "fire" in specific contexts, it reveals fathering characteristics.

There are two types of fire mentioned in the Old Testament. The first is what we normally think of when the word *fire* is used: a physical flame that burns and produces heat. This type of fire is used all over the Bible.

God desires for us to see ourselves through His eyes.

One of my son's favorite Biblical stories is about Shadrach, Meshach, and Abednego escaping the fiery furnace.

In that story, King Nebuchadnezzar had the furnace "heated seven times hotter than normal" (Daniel 3:19). It was so hot, in fact, that when the guards tossed the three men into the fire, they themselves were killed by its flames. The word *fire* in this context describes physical fire that burns and gives heat.

But there is another kind of fire mentioned in the Bible. One of the first times we see a fire that is not physical is when Moses happens upon a burning bush at "Horeb, the mountain of God" (Exodus 3:1). There Moses describes a bush filled with fire, yet not being consumed.

"There the angel of the Lord appeared to him in flames of fire from within a bush. Moses saw that though the bush was on fire it did not burn up. So Moses thought, 'I will go over and see this strange sight-why the bush does not burn up.' When the Lord saw that he had gone over to look, God called to him from within the bush, 'Moses! Moses!' And Moses said, 'Here I am.'" Exodus 3:2-4

This supernatural fiery phenomenon reoccurs from time to time throughout both the Old and New Testaments. When Moses went up Mount Sinai to retrieve the tablets of stone, it is recorded in Exodus 24:17, "To the Israelites the glory of the Lord looked like a consuming fire on top of the mountain." Yet when Moses came back down the mountain, Paul tells us that it was not smoke or the smell of charred flesh that rose from him, but the glory of the Lord (2 Corinthians 3:7). This fire was obviously not physical, but residue of the presence and glory of God.

When the disciples received the promised Holy Spirit at Pentecost, Luke tells us:

"They saw what seemed to be tongues of fire that separated and came to rest on each of them." Acts 2:3

This also was not physical fire, but again the visual evidence of God descending upon the first Christians.

This second type of fire is consistently used to describe God's glorious presence and activity in a specific location. We find it as that of a great pillar, when God leads His people from Egypt (Exodus 13:21), and the substance of His glory in the visions of His prophets (Ezekiel 1:4-27).

This fire, representing the presence and activity of God, is placed in the eye sockets of Jesus when He speaks to the church in Thyatira. This fire is not physical, but represents the type of sight in which Jesus sees the church. Jesus does not process this world through physical eyes, but through the wisdom and revelation of His Father.

This revelation of sight is evidenced by Jesus' insight into the identity of the woman He calls Jezebel. Like everyone else in the church, this woman had a name by which she was known. That name, however, did not describe her true identity. Her true identity was revealed by the One who saw through the eyes of His Heavenly Father.

Jesus' description of His eyes reveal to us how we, as Christians, are to see our world. Though we have a measure of wisdom and insight produced from our experiences in this world, it does not compare to the sight produced by our Father in Heaven. God wants us to see our world through His eyes. He wants us to rely on His sight.

Life looks different when we see through the eyes of the Holy Spirit. Everyday events, from driving in rush-hour traffic to disciplining our children, look different when we choose to rely on our Father's sight instead of our own. His perspective is right. His vantage point is true.

All that the church in Thyatira had suffered, under the deception and sin of Jezebel, resulted from men and women who chose not to see through the eyes of God their Father. This is the real consequence of sin. When a Christian tolerates sin corporately or personally, they forfeit the true perspective of God and gain the false perspective of the enemy.

FEET LIKE BURNISHED BRONZE

Jesus' description of His feet is very similar to that of His eyes. In the Bible, *glowing bronze* is found with spiritual significance. There is, of course, references to things made with the metal bronze, but in regards to our passage, the metal is hardly applicable to either Jesus' feet or consistent with the spiritual fiery eyes in which He sees. The reference to bronze in our passage has spiritual significance.

We find the spiritual meaning of Jesus' bronze feet in few different passages where both God and His Heavenly beings are depicted with possessing bronze features. In Ezekiel's vision of God's glory, recorded for us in Ezekiel 1:4-27, several of the celestial beings have bronze feet.

In his vision of one who looks strikingly similar to John's description of Jesus in Revelation 1:12-16, Daniel describes a man who not only had legs of bronze, but arms of bronze as well. He writes;

"His body was like chrysolite, his face like lightning, his eyes like flaming torches, his arms and legs like the gleam of burnished bronze, and his voice like the sound of a multitude." Daniel 10:6

Bronze is a hard and strong metal and used both physically and figuratively in the Bible. Its physical characteristics of strength and beauty reveal why it is often used to describe the supernatural. There would appear to be no better imagery to describe the strength, surety, and perfection of God than with this precious metal.

Jesus uses it in His address to the church in Thyatira to describe similar characteristics of a child of God. The feet of God's children are strong, their way is sure, and as Paul would say, "How beautiful are the feet of those who bring good news" (Romans 10:15).

Again we see the significance of Jesus' words when describing a child of God. Not only do God's children see with His eyes, they also walk in the strong, sure, and beautiful paths that their Father lays before them. It is no wonder why we read passages like Isaiah 54:17: "No weapon forged against you will prevail."

Our Father in Heaven has not left us to wander alone in this world, struggling to find our own way. He desires to be actively involved in the direction of our life. He is leading, forging a way for us to walk in victory, peace, and safety. He will never leave us and never forsake us! He is our Abba!

As I sit here and write of all I have discovered about the identity of a child of God, I wonder to myself if you are feeling the same way that I am. It is utterly overwhelming to embrace the Truth that God desires to be involved not only in the overarching plan to save us from Hell, but in the intimate details of our everyday life. He not only cares about the big stuff, but the small things as well.

> Our Father in Heaven has not left us to wander alone in this world, struggling to find our own way. He desires to be actively involved in the direction of our life.

I wonder, how does this passage change what you are currently facing in your life? If you read this book and leave it in the *churchy*, theological realm in which many Christians seem to walk in these days, then for you, this book is a complete waste of your time.

However, if you are authentically living as a child of God, not living in rebellion and sin, but walking with God as the loving Father He is, wouldn't that curb any situation that produces fear and doubt in your life? Wouldn't that put your mind at ease as you process the difficulties in which you are currently facing?

I may be the one writing this book, but I too feel the same pressures you feel. I fill up my gas tank just like you do. I wonder at times, just like you wonder, how the bills are going to get paid. We live in a world that is coming apart at the seams and everyone, Christian and pre-Christian[5] alike, feel the weight of that fact.

Yet as children of God, we have hope! We really do! We not only can believe, but know beyond a shadow of doubt that God is our Father and He is fathering us as we walk in this world. He is giving us

---

[5] "Pre-Christian" is the term I use to describe unbelievers. All people are pre-Christian until they respond to God's gift of salvation and become Christian. It's a perspective every Christian should have of unsaved people.

eyes to see and feet to walk. He is showing us His perspective and providing the surety and strength to walk in that perspective.

I will be praying for you, the one who is reading this book. I pray that you will walk with God as a child walks with his father. I pray you will become more familiar with His voice, and as you learn to process life with Him, you will live all the more confident and in peace. I ask this of God our Father, on your behalf, in the name of Jesus our Brother. Amen.

KEY CONCEPTS

God desires His relationship with us to be the same as His relationship with Jesus. That relationship is best illustrated in the parent-child context.

The relationship between God the Father and God the Son mark the beginning of human existence. In the foreknowledge of God, He predestined human beings to be His children just as Jesus is His only begotten Son.

Since Christianity is relational, sin is also relational.

How we see ourselves determines how we live our life. When we embrace our identity as a child of God, we also embrace all that God has destined for Jesus Himself.

When we choose to see with "Eyes like Blazing Fire" and walk with "Feet like Burnished Bronze" we choose to see our world through the eyes of Jesus and walk in victory just like Jesus did.

REFLECTION QUESTIONS

1. What is the root of sin?

2. How does the Bible compare our parenting to the parenting of God?

3. What happened in the parent/child relationship when Adam sinned? What exactly changed?

4. Have you ever felt like the Prodigal Son? We all have. Why is this story significant?

5. Why is it important for us to see ourselves as Jesus saw Himself - a child of God?

6. What happens when we see the world through the Father's eyes?